U.S. Federal Courts:
Attorney Admission Requirements

2011 Edition

John Okray

Lawyerup Press LLC
P.O. Box 156148
Fort Worth, TX 76155
Fax: (888) 672-2833
editor@lawyeruppress.com
www.lawyeruppress.com

Library of Congress Control Number: 2010912706

ISBN-13: 978-0-9829658-0-1

To Sophie, Ashlyn, Kelly, Dorothy and Jennifer:

For their indulgence of my idiosyncrasies and
their support in all my endeavors.

U.S. Federal Courts:
Attorney Admission Requirements

2011 Edition by John Okray   © Lawyerup Press LLC

Table of Contents

About the Author

John Okray serves as Assistant General Counsel of a financial services firm in Texas. He received his BA in political science from the University of Massachusetts Boston, a JD from Suffolk University Law School, an MBA from the Suffolk University Sawyer School of Management, and an LLM in taxation from Boston University School of Law. He has served on various public service and non-profit boards and is active in organized bar activities.

Photos

All photos referencing U.S. sources were from U.S. federal government agency websites, however, credit has been provided to the agency and photographer where known. Works of the United States Federal Government are in the public domain under Title 17, Chapter 1, Section 105 of the US Code. Wikipedia photos were designated as being in the public domain by the contributors. Acronyms in photo sources used include:

GSA: General Services Administration; DOJ: Department of Justice; DOE: Department of Energy; FBI: Federal Bureau of Investigation; LC: Library of Congress; NGA: National Gallery of Art; PO: Probation Office

Cover Photograph: Franz Jantzen, *Collection of the Supreme Court of the United States*.

Improving Future Editions:

The author intends to write periodic editions of this book to expand the content and provided updated admission requirements. Therefore, any feedback would be greatly appreciated. Comments and suggestions may be submitted to the publisher:

Lawyerup Press LLC
P.O. Box 156148
Fort Worth, TX 76155
Fax: (888) 672-2833
editor@lawyeruppress.com
www.lawyeruppress.com

Disclaimer

Preface

While one might be inclined to think the rules for bar admission across the U.S. federal court system would be uniform, this is simply not the case. There are numerous examples of varying admission criteria and procedures, even within the same circuit, the same state or the same judicial district. In some federal courts an attorney who is a member in good standing of any state bar could be admitted in a matter of days with minimal effort and little to no expense. Conversely, other courts have independent examinations, initial and recurring fees, sponsorship requirements, etc.

The primary purpose for writing this book is to provide a straightforward guide for attorneys who may seek admission to any of the federal courts. The book will answer questions, such as:

- Do I need to be a member of the state bar to be admitted to the U.S. District Court?
- Which federal courts have reciprocity?
- Does District Court admission automatically provide membership in its Bankruptcy Court?
- Does the court allow *pro hac vice* admissions?
- What are the admission and renewal fees, if any?
- Do I have to take an exam or any courses to be admitted to the court?
- Are there any continuing legal education requirements for members?
- Do I need an attorney to sponsor my motion for admission?
- Must the oath be given in person in open court?
- Are there any residency requirements for membership?
- Do I need to be in the military to be admitted to a particular military court of appeals?
- What courts allow non-attorneys or attorneys licensed outside the U.S. to be members?
- What are the admission rules for the U.S. territorial courts?
- What are the admission rules for the courts of the freely associated states?

Anyone considering a multijurisdictional practice that involves the practice of law in the federal court system should find this information useful.

There is also an educational purpose for this book. The more research I conducted, the more intrigued I became by the differences and peculiarities in the rules of admission in the federal court system. *U.S. Federal Courts: Attorney Admission Requirements* and future editions will provide not only a snapshot in time, but also a historical record of a transition to more a liberal or restrictive admission framework.

John Okray

Overview

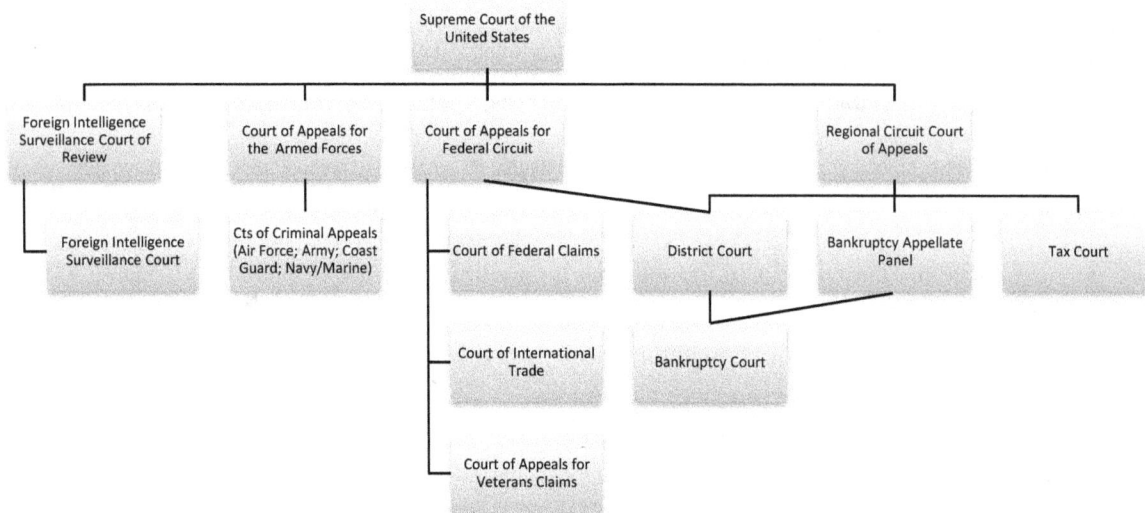

U.S. Court	Article	Judicial Term
Supreme Court	III	Life
Regional Courts of Appeals	III	Life
Court of Appeals for the Federal Circuit	III	Life
Court of International Trade	III	Life
District Courts (incl. DC and Puerto Rico)	III	Life
Foreign Intelligence Surveillance Court & Court of Review	III	7 Years
Court of Federal Claims	I	15 Years
Bankruptcy Courts	I	14 Years
Territorial District Courts (Virgin Islands, Guam, Northern Mariana Islands)	IV	10 Years
Court of Appeals for the Armed Forces	I	15 Years
Military Courts of Criminal Appeals	I	Not Fixed
Court of Appeals for Veterans Claims	I	15 Years
Tax Court	I	15 Years

2011 Edition by John Okray   © Lawyerup Press LLC

Supreme Court of the United States

Article III of the Constitution:
The judicial power of the United States, shall be vested in one supreme Court, and in such inferior Court as the Congress may from time to time ordain and establish...

The Supreme Court of the United States is the highest court in the judicial branch of government. The Court only has original and exclusive jurisdiction in controversies between two or more states. In most cases the Court exercises discretionary appellate jurisdiction. Justices are appointed by the President and confirmed by the Senate to a lifetime term. There are no appeals from the Supreme Court. The Court is based in Washington, D.C.

Photograph by Franz Jantzen, Collection of the Supreme Court of the United States

U.S. Regional Circuit Courts of Appeal

The United States District Courts are divided into twelve regional circuits, with each circuit having its own U.S. Court of Appeals. Regional Courts of Appeals hear appeals from District Courts and Bankruptcy Appellate Panels within their judicial circuit and appeals from the U.S. Tax Court. The regional U.S. Courts of Appeals are Article III courts. Judges are appointed by the President and confirmed by the Senate to a lifetime term. Appeals from the regional Courts of Appeals are heard infrequently by the Supreme Court of the United States. Each regional circuit court of appeals is located within its judicial circuit.

U.S. District Courts

The United States District Courts have jurisdiction to hear cases on almost any federal subject matter, whether civil or criminal. There is at least one district court in each of the states, the District of Columbia, and Puerto Rico (see also Territorial Courts). These District Courts are Article III courts. Judges are appointed by the President and confirmed by the Senate to a lifetime term. Appeals from the District Courts are heard by the applicable U.S. Circuit Court of Appeals. Each federal judicial district has one or more District Courts located within it, including a main court for the district.

U.S. Bankruptcy Courts & U.S. Bankruptcy Appellate Panels

U.S. Bankruptcy Courts
Each of the federal judicial districts handles bankruptcy matters as the federal courts have exclusive jurisdiction over these cases. In almost all federal districts bankruptcy cases are heard by a separate Bankruptcy Court. The Bankruptcy Courts are Article I courts established by Congress. Bankruptcy Court Judges are appointed by a majority of judges from the regional U.S. Circuit Court of Appeals to a term of fourteen years. Appeals from a Bankruptcy Court are heard by its associated District Court, or the Bankruptcy Appellate Panel if the circuit established one. Bankruptcy Courts are located within their associated federal judicial district.

U.S. Bankruptcy Appellate Panels
The regional federal judicial circuits may establish Bankruptcy Appellate Panels to hear appeals from Bankruptcy Courts located in the circuit. Bankruptcy Court Judges are appointed to serve on Bankruptcy Appellate Panels. Appeals from a Bankruptcy Appellate Panel are heard by the regional U.S. Circuit Court of Appeals. Currently the First, Sixth, Eighth, Ninth and Tenth Circuits have Bankruptcy Appellate Panels. Bankruptcy Appellate Panels are located within their associated federal judicial circuit.

U.S. Courts of Specific Subject-Matter Jurisdiction

U.S. Court of Appeals for the Federal Circuit

The United States Court of Appeals for the Federal Circuit is an Article III court established by Congress. Judges are appointed by the President and confirmed by the Senate to a lifetime term. The Court hears appeals from the U.S. Court of Federal Claims, the U.S. Court of International Trade and the U.S. Court of Appeals for Veterans Claims. The Court also hears appeals from U.S. District Courts related to patents and trademarks. Appeals from the Court are heard infrequently by the Supreme Court of the United States. The Court is based in Washington, D.C.

U.S. Court of International Trade

The United States Court of International Trade is an Article III court. Judges are appointed by the President and confirmed by the Senate to a lifetime term. The Court hears cases against the United States relating to international trade and associated counterclaims, as well as civil actions brought by the United States relating to customs transactions. Appeals from the Court are heard by the United States Court of Appeals for the Federal Circuit. The Court is based in New York City.

U.S. Court of Federal Claims

The United States Court of Federal Claims is an Article I court established by Congress. Judges are appointed by the President and confirmed by the Senate to a term of fifteen years. The Court hears most claims for monetary damages against the United States, such as compensation for the taking of private property or damages for breach of contract. Appeals from the Court are heard by the United States Court of Appeals for the Federal Circuit. The Court is based in Washington, D.C.

U.S. Tax Court

The United States Tax Court is an Article I court established by Congress. Judges are appointed by the President and confirmed by the Senate to a term of fifteen years. The Court reviews determinations made by the Commissioner of Internal Revenue related to tax deficiencies and other tax matters. One of the notable aspects of the Court is that a taxpayer may defer payment of the disputed amount until the Court has rendered its decision. Appeals from the Court are heard by the applicable regional Circuit Court of Appeals. The Court is based in Washington, D.C.

U.S. Court of Appeals for the Armed Forces

The United States Court of Appeals for the Armed Forces is an Article I court established by Congress. The Court's civilian judges are appointed by the President and confirmed by the Senate to a term of fifteen years. The Court hears cases related to active-duty members of the armed forces and individuals subject to the Uniform Code of Military Justice, including certain appeals from the four intermediate military courts of criminal appeals. In certain criminal matters, Servicemembers are entitled to military counsel, but may also be represented by civilian counsel at their own expense. Appeals from the Court are heard by the Supreme Court of the United States. The Court is based in Washington, D.C.

U.S. Court of Appeals for Veterans Claims

The United States Court of Appeals for Veterans Claims is an Article I court established by Congress. Judges are appointed by the President and confirmed by the Senate to a term of fifteen years. The Court hears appeals of determinations of the Board of Veterans' Appeals related to benefit claims. Appeals from the Court are heard by the United States Court of Appeals for the Federal Circuit. The Court is based in Washington, D.C.

Foreign Intelligence Surveillance Court of Review

The United States Foreign Intelligence Surveillance Court of Review was established by Congress and hears appeals from the Foreign Intelligence Surveillance Court. The Chief Justice of the Supreme Court of the United States appoints three judges to the Court, chosen from the U.S. District Court and Court of Appeals judges. Judges are appointed for a term of seven years and are not eligible for reappointment. Appeals from the Court are heard by the Supreme Court of the United States.

Foreign Intelligence Surveillance Court

The United States Foreign Intelligence Surveillance Court was established by Congress and hears applications from the United States federal government for physical searches or electronic surveillance seeking to obtain foreign intelligence information. This information is sought by the government to prevent crimes such as espionage or terrorism. Eleven U.S. District Court judges are appointed by the Chief Justice of the Supreme Court of the United States to this Court. Judges are appointed for a term of seven years and are not eligible for reappointment. Appeals are heard by the Foreign Intelligence Court of Review. The Court is based in Washington, D.C.

District of Columbia Courts

The District of Columbia is a federal district and the United States Capitol. The courts in the District Court that are equivalent to state courts are the Superior Court of the District of Columbia and the District of Columbia Court of Appeals. The Superior Court of the District of Columbia is the trial court of general jurisdiction and the District of Columbia Court of Appeals is the highest court for the district akin to a state supreme court.

The District of Columbia also has an Article III U.S. District Court akin to those in the states and the Commonwealth of Puerto Rico. District Court Judges are appointed by the President and confirmed by the Senate to a lifetime term. Appeals from the District Court are heard by the U.S. Court of Appeals for the District of Columbia Circuit.

The District of Columbia is also home to numerous federal courts with national jurisdiction.

Territorial Courts

Puerto Rico
(see also U.S. District Courts)
The Commonwealth of Puerto Rico is a territory of the United States located in the Caribbean Sea. The Supreme Court of Puerto Rico is the highest territorial court. Puerto Rico has an Article III U.S. District Court akin to those in the states and the District of Columbia. District Court Judges are appointed by the President and confirmed by the Senate to a lifetime term. Appeals from the District Court are heard by the U.S. Court of Appeals for the First Circuit.

U.S. Virgin Islands
The United States Virgin Islands is a territory of the United States located in the Caribbean Sea. The Supreme Court of the United States Virgin Islands is the highest territorial court. The United States Virgin Islands has an Article IV District Court. Judges of the District Court are appointed by the President and confirmed by the Senate to a term of fourteen years. Appeals from the District Court are heard by the U.S. Court of Appeals for the Third Circuit.

Guam
Guam is a territory of the United States located in the Pacific Ocean. The highest territorial court is the Supreme Court of Guam. Guam has an Article IV District Court. Judges of the District Court are appointed by the President and confirmed by the Senate to a term of fourteen years. Appeals from the District Court are heard by the U.S. Court of Appeals for the Ninth Circuit.

Northern Mariana Islands
The Commonwealth of Northern Mariana Islands is a territory of the United States located in the Pacific Ocean. The Supreme Court of the Commonwealth of the Northern Mariana Islands is the highest territorial court. The Commonwealth of the Northern Mariana Islands has an Article IV District Court. Judges of the District Court are appointed by the President and confirmed by the Senate to a term of fourteen years. Appeals from the District Court are heard by the U.S. Court of Appeals for the Ninth Circuit.

American Samoa
American Samoa is a territory of the United States located in the South Pacific Ocean. The High Court of American Samoa is the highest court in the territory. Justices are appointed by the United States Secretary of the Interior from recommendations of the Governor. There is no U.S. District Court in American Samoa.

Courts of the Freely Associated States

Marshall Islands

The Republic of the Marshall Islands is a sovereign state in the Pacific Ocean, which was formerly administered by the United States on behalf of the United Nations. The Republic of the Marshall Islands has entered into Compact of Free Association with the United States. While the Republic of the Marshall Islands is an independent state, there remains considerable economic, political and military defense coordination between it and the United States. The highest court is the Supreme Court of the Republic of the Marshall Islands.

Micronesia

The Federated States of Micronesia is a sovereign state in the Pacific Ocean, which was formerly administered by the United States on behalf of the United Nations. The Federated States of Micronesia has entered into Compact of Free Association with the United States. While the Federated States of Micronesia is an independent state, there remains considerable economic, political and military defense coordination between it and the United States. The highest court is the Supreme Court of the Federated States of Micronesia.

Palau

The Republic of Palau is a sovereign state in the Pacific Ocean, which was formerly administered by the United States on behalf of the United Nations. The Republic of Palau has entered into Compact of Free Association with the United States. While the Republic of Palau is an independent state, there remains considerable economic, political and military defense coordination between it and the United States. The highest court is the Supreme Court of the Republic of Palau.

Court Specific Admission Requirements and Guide

Please take the following factors into consideration when reading the court specific admissions information that follows.

Addresses: When a court lists a specific address for attorney admission applications it has been provided. Otherwise, the address for the Clerk of the Court at the court's main office is listed. Many courts that require an oath to be administered in person may allow the applicant to appear before a court located within the judicial district other than the main court listed. Contact the Court Clerk for locations.

Authorized Active Judges: The number of authorized judgeships for each U.S. court is determined by Congress. This information is provided for the Circuit and District Courts to gauge the relative size and scope of the courts. However, in addition to Authorized Judges, the courts also have Senior Judges and Magistrate Judges who handle a large volume of cases.

Attorneys Representing the Government: Many U.S. Courts waive certain admission requirements and fees for attorneys representing the United States. The territorial courts may have similar waivers in place for attorneys representing the government or in certain public service roles. Contact the Court Clerk for details.

Bar Associations: There are a number of voluntary bar associations geared toward attorneys who may practice in a particular U.S. Court, federal practice area or jurisdiction. These associations are meant to provide educational and other benefits to attorneys who practice in those areas but generally have no formal affiliation with the U.S. Courts. Some of the territorial courts may have compulsory bar membership. The inclusion of bar associations in this book is for informational purposes only and is not an endorsement of any bar association or its activities.

Certificate of Good Standing: These are issued by the Court upon request of a member typically for a nominal fee. Courts will often require an applicant to its bar to provide a Certificate of Good Standing from another court where the applicant is already admitted. In rare instances a court may require Certificates of Good Standing from all bars/courts where an applicant has been admitted.

Clerk of Court: The Clerk is an officer typically appointed by the judges of the court to handle the administrative affairs of the court. These may include maintaining records, handling financial matters, coordinating attorney admissions and other support to the court.

Discipline: It should be assumed that if someone if admitted to a Court, whether regular or *pro hac vice*, that the Court will assert jurisdiction to discipline that person for violations of its rules.

Examinations, Experience & Continuing Legal Education: Most federal courts do not have independent examinations, experience or continuing legal education requirements. However, a minority of federal courts may impose their own requirements, including but not limited to an examination, requirement for specific legal experience, or participation in a seminar or other relevant legal education. These requirements are subject to change at any time.

Fees: The fees listed are generally those for initial admission to the bar of a particular court. Many U.S. Courts charge an initial admission fee which is valid for life without any further requirements. Some courts also require members to pay periodic renewal fees. Fees and renewal policies are subject to change at any time. As previously noted, some courts may grant fee waivers or reductions for certain types of attorneys, including attorneys representing the government, public service attorneys, attorneys appointed under the Criminal Justice Act, attorneys who are active-duty members of the U.S. military, etc.

Honorary Members: Some courts are allowed to grant honorary memberships to its bar. These honorary memberships are typically akin to honorary degrees from a university and do not generally entail the right to practice law before that court.

Law Student Practice: Many courts have rules that allow law students to assist attorneys in trials. Contact the Court Clerk for details.

Local Rules: Many of the local rules on admissions have been included, but due to space limitations, in most cases they have been abbreviated and not copied verbatim. Therefore, you should refer to the actual local rules if seeking admission to determine whether any special rules apply to your situation.

Magistrate Judges: Magistrate Judges are appointed by a majority of the District Court Judges to serve a term of eight years if full-time or four years if part-time. Certain matters in the District Courts may be heard by Magistrate Judges.

Member/Active/Good Standing: An applicant admitted through the regular admission process to a Court is considered a member of the bar of that court. When a court requires an applicant or sponsor to be a "member" of a particular bar, it should generally be assumed this means an 1) active member of that bar, 2) currently in good standing in all jurisdictions where admitted, 3) that has not been subject to disciplinary action by that or any other bar.

Pro Hac Vice: Admission *pro hac vice* means an attorney is seeking temporary admission typically for a particular case. Most federal courts allow an attorney to be admitted *pro hac vice* without seeking permanent admission, but the requirements vary widely in terms of the fees, procedures and limitations. A minority of federal courts allows *pro hac vice* admission only for extremely compelling circumstances at the discretion of the judge or they may not allow *pro hac vice* admissions at all.

Senior Judges: Generally, a federal judge who has reached the age of at least 65 and has served for a minimum of 15 years may continue to serve as a judge under senior status. A Senior Judge no longer occupies one of the court's authorized judgeship seats.

Sponsor: In most cases where an applicant is required to have one or more sponsors, the sponsor is typically required to be an active member in good standing of that same court. Some courts allow sponsors to be from different courts or the courts may forego the necessity for a sponsor if the applicant provides a Certificate of Good Standing from another court. Some courts require the sponsor make a motion for the applicant's admission in writing or in person before a judge of that court.

State: When it references an applicant must be a member of the state court, it should be assumed this means admitted to practice before the highest court of that state. Unless otherwise stated, state should be assumed to mean state within in the United States and not a foreign sovereign state.

Telephone Numbers: For the District Courts, where the court has listed a phone number for bar applicants to call with questions, that number has been provided. Otherwise the phone number for the main office of the District Court is listed. For the other courts, the general phone number for the main office is given.

Territory: Whenever it states an applicant may be a member of a "territory" court, this would typically include the Commonwealth of Puerto Rico, the U.S. Virgin Islands, the Commonwealth of the Northern Mariana Islands, and Guam. Applicants should confirm this with the Court Clerk.

Websites: The websites for the various courts have been provided so potential applicants can search for application forms, confirm admission rules and requirements, etc.

Supreme Court of the United States

Courtroom photograph by Franz Jantzen
Collection of the Supreme Court of the United States

Admission

Bar/Court Membership Required	Any U.S. state, commonwealth, territory, possession or District of Columbia in good standing for at least 3 years immediately before application
Additional Test Required	No
Certificate of Good Standing Required	Yes, and personal statement
Sponsor Required	Yes (2)
Oath Required	Yes
Fee	$200

Pro Hac Vice Admission

An attorney not admitted to practice in the highest court of a State, Commonwealth, Territory or Possession, or the District of Columbia for the requisite three years, but otherwise eligible for admission to practice in this Court, may be permitted to argue *pro hac vice*.
An attorney qualified to practice in the courts of a foreign state may be permitted to argue *pro hac vice*.
Oral argument *pro hac vice* is allowed only on motion of the counsel of record for the party on whose behalf leave is requested. The motion shall state concisely the qualifications of the attorney who is to argue *pro hac vice*. It shall be filed with the Clerk, in the form required under the Rules, no later than the date on which the respondent's or appellee's brief on the merits is due to be filed, and it shall be accompanied by proof of service as required under the Rules.

Address
Clerk, Supreme Court of the United States
1 First Street, N.E.
Washington, D.C. 20543-0001

Telephone
202-479-3387
Court Website
www.supremecourt.gov

U.S. Court of Appeals for the First Circuit

Authorized Active Judges	Circuit
6	1

John Joseph Moakley United States Courthouse. Photos: U.S. NGA / GSA; Anonymous on Wikipedia

Admission

Bar/Court Membership Required	Any state, another U.S. Court of Appeals, Supreme Court of the United States, a U.S. District Court (including U.S. Virgin Islands, the Northern Mariana Islands, and Guam)
Additional Test Required	No
Certificate of Good Standing Required	Yes, from any state bar
Sponsor Required	Yes
Oath Required	Yes
Fee	$200

Address
United States Court of Appeals
1 Courthouse Way
Suite 2500
Boston, MA 02210

Telephone
617-748-9057

Appeals Court Website
www.ca1.uscourts.gov

16

U.S. District Court - Maine

Authorized Active Judges	Circuit
3	1

Edward T. Gignoux U.S. Courthouse. Photo: U.S. GSA

Admission

State Bar Membership Required	Maine
Automatic Admission with State Bar Membership	No
Additional Test Required	No
Certificate of Good Standing Required	No
Sponsor Required	Yes, in person
Oath Required	Yes
Fee	$150

Pro Hac Vice Admission

Leave of Court is granted to any attorney who is not a member of the bar of this Court to practice in this Court provided the attorney files with the Clerk a certificate for admission to be admitted *pro hac vice* for each case. The attorney must file a form certifying that he/she is admitted to practice in any other U.S. federal court or any State and is not currently under any order of disbarment, suspension or any other discipline in any court of record in the U.S. and that no proceedings that might lead to such discipline are pending.

The Clerk shall cause to be made such an investigation of the requesting attorney's eligibility as necessary. Any such attorney shall have at all times associated with him/her a member of the bar of this Court. $100 fee.

Address
Clerk, U.S. District Court
156 Federal Street
Portland, ME 04101

Telephone
207-945-0575
District Court Website
www.med.uscourts.gov

Bankruptcy Court Admission

Regular: Members of the bar of the U.S. District Court for the District of Maine may practice before this Court.

Pro Hac Vice: No fee for *pro hac vice* admission.

Bankruptcy Court Website
www.meb.uscourts.gov

Telephone
207-780-3482

U.S. District Court – Massachusetts

Authorized Active Judges	Circuit
13	1

Admission

Commonwealth Bar Membership Required	Massachusetts
Automatic Admission with Commonwealth Bar Membership	No
Additional Test Required	No
Certificate of Good Standing Required	Yes
Sponsor Required	No
Oath Required	Yes, in person
Fee	$200

Pro Hac Vice Admission

In order to be admitted to the bar of this court *pro hac vice*, a motion must first be filed in the action in which the attorney seeks to be admitted. The motion cannot be filed by the attorney seeking admission, but must be signed and filed by a member of the bar of this court. Note, it is the duty of the moving attorney to first verify the bar admission status of the attorney he or she is sponsoring for admission to the court *pro hac vice*.

The motion must be accompanied by an affidavit stating the attorney is a member in good standing in every jurisdiction where admitted to practice, there are no disciplinary proceedings pending and the attorney is familiar with the Local Rules of the Court.

A $ 50 fee is required with the filing of the motion for the attorney seeking admission. The fee is not refundable should the motion be denied.

Address
Bar Liaison - Suite 2300
United States District Court
John Joseph Moakley U.S. Courthouse
1 Courthouse Way
Boston, MA 02210

Telephone
617-748-9165

District Court Website
www.mad.uscourts.gov

Bankruptcy Court Admission

Regular: A person who is a member of the bar of U.S. District Court for the District of Massachusetts may appear and practice before this Court.

Pro Hac Vice: An attorney who is not a member of the bar of the U.S. District Court for the District of Massachusetts, but is a member of the bar of any other U.S. District Court or the bar of any state may appear and practice in this Court in a particular case or adversary proceeding only by leave granted in the discretion of the Court, provided such attorney files a certificate attesting that (1) the attorney is a member of the bar in good standing in every jurisdiction where the attorney has been admitted to practice; (2) there are no disciplinary proceedings pending against such attorney as a member of the bar in any jurisdiction; and (3) the attorney is familiar with the Local Rules of this Court. [Additional rules and exceptions apply] No fee.

Bankruptcy Court Website
www.mab.uscourts.gov

Telephone
617-748-5300

U.S. District Court – New Hampshire

Authorized Active Judges	Circuit
3	1

Admission

State Bar Membership Required	New Hampshire
Automatic Admission with State Bar Membership	No
Additional Test Required	No
Certificate of Good Standing Required	No, U.S. Attorney will review eligibility
Sponsor Required	If the U.S. Attorney for the Dist. of New Hampshire determines the applicant is eligible, a representative from that office shall move for the applicant's admission. If the U.S. Attorney is not satisfied, any member of the bar of this court may move for the applicant's admission, and the U.S. Attorney or an assistant may oppose the motion. If the U.S. Attorney files an objection, the clerk's office shall advise the applicant. Unless the applicant withdraws the application, the court shall conduct a hearing on the application.
Oath Required	Yes, in person
Fee	$180

Pro Hac Vice Admission

Requirements:
1. be a member in good standing of the bar of any court of the United States or the highest court of any state;
2. have a member of the bar of this district who is actively associated with the attorney seeking admission file a motion for *pro hac vice* admission;
3. attach to the motion an affidavit from the attorney seeking *pro hac vice* admission;
4. submit with the motion the $100 fee to the Clerk.

Address
U.S. District Court, District of New Hampshire
55 Pleasant Street, Room 110
Concord, NH 03301-3941

Telephone
603-225-1423
District Court Website
www.nhd.uscourts.gov

Bankruptcy Court Admission

Regular: Attorneys admitted to the bar of the U.S. District Court for the District of New Hampshire are admitted to practice before the Bankruptcy Court.
Pro Hac Vice: Any attorney not admitted to the bar of the U.S. District Court of New Hampshire may appear and practice before the Bankruptcy Court in a particular action at the Court's discretion and on motion by a member of the bar of the U.S. District Court of New Hampshire who is actively associated with him or her in a particular action.   No fee.

Bankruptcy Court Website
www.nhb.uscourts.gov

Telephone
603-222-2600

U.S. District Court – Puerto Rico

Authorized Active Judges	Circuit
7	1

Admission

Commonwealth Bar Required	Any U.S. State, District of Columbia or Territory
Automatic Admission with Commonwealth Bar Membership	No
Additional Test Required	Yes, Federal Bar Examination (see Local Rule 83A for exceptions)
Certificate of Good Standing Required	Yes, from bar where attorney is admitted, as well as "certificate of good conduct" from police department where the attorney resides
Sponsor Required	Must provide 3 references including 2 bar members who are Puerto Rico residents. The Committee on Admissions sends recommendation to Court and the active judges vote on admission.
Oath Required	Yes
Fee	$200 (plus $100 exam fee). Annual renewal is $50.

Pro Hac Vice Admission

An attorney who does not reside in the Commonwealth of Puerto Rico and who is authorized to practice law before the bar of any U.S. court or of the highest court of any state, the District of Columbia, Puerto Rico, Guam, the Northern Mariana Islands or the U.S. Virgin Islands, may apply for permission to appear as attorney of record in a particular case. The movant shall:
(1) designate a member of the bar of this Court as local counsel;
(2) state the court(s) in which the movant is admitted to practice law;
(3) attest that the movant is not suspended from practicing before any court or jurisdiction;
(4) state if any complaint for unethical misconduct, disciplinary proceeding, or criminal charges involving the movant are currently pending before any court or jurisdiction; and,
(5) pay the $150 fee (per appearance).

Address
Federico Degetau Federal Building,
150 Carlos Chardón Street
San Juan, Puerto Rico 00918-1767

Telephone
787-772-3018
District Court Website
www.prd.uscourts.gov

Bankruptcy Court Admission

Regular: Attorneys admitted to the bar of the U.S. District Court for the District of Puerto Rico may practice in this court.
Pro hac Vice: An attorney may appear *pro hac vice* without a local attorney if the matter is uncontested, with the exception of representation as counsel to a debtor or trustee. However, if the matter is, or becomes contested, local counsel must enter an appearance at least five 5 days before the scheduled hearing. $150 fee (per appearance).

Bankruptcy Court Website
www.prb.uscourts.gov

Telephone
787-977-6000

U.S. District Court – Rhode Island

Authorized Active Judges	Circuit
3	1

Federal Building & U.S. Courthouse. Photo: National Archives, RG 121-BS, Box 79, Folder M

Admission

State Bar Membership Required	Rhode Island
Automatic Admission with State Bar	No
Additional Test Required	No, but course on federal practice is mandatory
Cert. of Good Standing Required	Yes, Rhode Island **and** any U.S. District Court(s)
Sponsor Required	Motion is made by Chairman of Board of Bar Adm.
Oath Required	Yes
Fee	$150. Membership must be renewed every 4 years.

Pro Hac Vice Admission

In order to be eligible for *pro hac vice* admission, an applicant must:
(1) Be a member of the bar of another state and another federal district court and the bar in every jurisdiction in which the attorney has been admitted to practice; and
(2) Establish, to the satisfaction of this Court, that he or she is otherwise qualified and fit to be admitted to practice *pro hac vice* before this Court. $50 fee.

Address
U.S. District Court
One Exchange Place
Providence, RI 02903

Telephone
401-752-7200
District Court Website
www.rid.uscourts.gov

Bankruptcy Court Admission

Regular: An attorney who is in good standing of the bar of the Supreme Court of Rhode Island and is admitted to practice in the U.S. District Court for the District of Rhode Island shall be deemed admitted to practice in this Court.
Pro Hac Vice: A member of the bar of any state and the bar of any other U.S. District Court may, upon motion, be permitted to try a particular case. With the exception of representation as counsel to a debtor or trustee, an attorney may appear *pro hac vice* without a local attorney if the matter is uncontested. If the matter is or becomes contested, then local counsel must enter an appearance at least 7 days before the hearing. $50 fee.

Bankruptcy Court Website
www.rib.uscourts.gov

Telephone
401-626-3100

Bankruptcy Appellate Panel for the First Circuit

Admission

An attorney is admitted to practice before the before the Bankruptcy Panel for the First Circuit if the attorney is:

(1) admitted to practice by and a member in good standing of the United States Court of Appeals for the First Circuit,
(2) admitted to practice by and a member in good standing of a United States District Court within the First Circuit, or
(3) admitted to practice by a United States Bankruptcy Court in the case or proceeding on appeal.

Pro Hac Vice Admission

Any attorney not admitted to practice by the United States Court of Appeals for the First Circuit, a United States District Court within the First Circuit, or a United States Bankruptcy Court in the case or proceeding on appeal may, upon a motion, appear and practice before the BAP in a particular action at the BAP's discretion. All such motions shall have attached a supporting affidavit containing:

(1) the attorney's address, telephone number, and facsimile number,
(2) a listing of the court(s) to which the attorney has been admitted to practice and the date(s) of admission,
(3) a statement that the attorney is in good standing and eligible to practice in the court(s),
(4) a statement that the attorney is not currently suspended or disbarred in any jurisdiction,
(5) a statement describing the nature and status of any pending disciplinary matters involving the attorney, and
(6) a statement that the attorney is familiar with the requirements of Rule VIII of the Rules of Attorney Disciplinary Enforcement for the Court of Appeals for the 1st Circuit.
No fee.

Address
U.S. Bankruptcy Appellate Panel for the First Circuit
John Joseph Moakley United States Courthouse
1 Courthouse Way, Suite 2500
Boston, MA 02210

Telephone
617-748-4774

BAP Website
www.bap1.uscourts.gov

U.S. Court of Appeals for the Second Circuit

Authorized Active Judges	Circuit
13	2

Thurgood Marshall U.S. Courthouse. Photos: U.S. GSA

Admission

Bar/Court Membership Required	Any state, another U.S. Court of Appeals, Supreme Court of the United States, or a U.S. District Court
Additional Test Required	No
Certificate of Good Standing Required	Yes
Sponsor Required	Yes
Oath Required	Yes
Fee	$190. Renew every 5 years for $25.

Address
United States Court of Appeals for the Second Circuit
40 Foley Square
New York, NY 10007

Federal Bar Council
www.federalbarcouncil.org

Telephone
212-857-8500

Court Website
www.ca2.uscourts.gov

U.S. District Court – Connecticut

Authorized Active Judges	Circuit
8	2

Abram Ribicoff Federal Building. Photo: U.S. Dist. Ct. of Connecticut

Admission

State Bar Membership Required	State of Connecticut or any U.S. District Court
Automatic Admission with State Bar Membership	No
Additional Test Required	No
Certificate of Good Standing Required	Yes, from Connecticut state court, Connecticut bar association, state wide grievance committee or another federal district court
Sponsor Required	Yes, 2 members of this bar that have known applicant for at least 6 months
Oath Required	Yes, in person
Fee	$160

Pro Hac Vice Admission

Lawyers not members of the Bar of this Court who are members in good standing of the bar of another Federal or State Court may be permitted to represent clients in criminal, civil and miscellaneous proceedings in this Court on written motion by a member of this Court.
The motion shall be accompanied by an affidavit, duly sworn and executed by the proposed visiting lawyer. See Local Rules for requirements. $25 fee.

Address
Office of the Clerk
U.S. District Court
450 Main Street
Hartford, CT 06103

Telephone
860-240-3200

District Court Website
www.ctd.uscourts.gov

Bankruptcy Court Admission

See District Court rules above. $25 fee for *pro hac vice* admissio*n.*

Bankruptcy Court Website
www.ctb.uscourts.gov

Telephone
860-240-3675

U.S. District Court – New York Eastern District

Authorized Active Judges	Circuit
15	2

Admission

State Bar Membership Required	New York, or a member of the U.S. District Court in Connecticut or Vermont and of the State bar in which such district court is located, provided such district court extends the same privilege to members of this court.
Auto Admission w/ State Bar	No
Additional Test Required	No
Certificate of Good Standing Required	Yes, from **each** state where a member
Sponsor Required	Yes
Oath Required	Yes
Fee	$170

Pro Hac Vice Admission

A member of the bar of any state or of any U.S. District Court may be permitted to try a particular case, upon motion and filing a certificate of the court for **each** of the states in which the applicant is a member of the bar, which has been issued within 30 days. $25 fee.

Address
U.S. District Court
225 Cadman Plaza East
Brooklyn, NY 11201

Telephone
718-613-2285

District Court Website
www.nyed.uscourts.gov

Conrad B. Duberstein U.S. Bankruptcy Courthouse. Photo: U.S. GSA

Bankruptcy Court Admission

Regular: Members of the U.S. District Court for the Eastern District of New York.

Pro Hac Vice: Upon motion made, a member of the bar of any state or of any U.S. District Court may be permitted to practice in this Court in a particular case. When involvement in the case is limited to filing a notice of appearance under Bankruptcy Rule 2002, filing a proof of claim or interest, or representing a child support creditor, you may appear for those purposes without obtaining authorization to appear *pro hac vice*. $25 fee.

Bankruptcy Court Website
www.nyeb.uscourts.gov

Telephone
347-394-1700

U.S. District Court – New York Northern District

Authorized Active Judges	Circuit
5	2

James T. Foley U.S. Post Office & Courthouse. Photos: U.S. GSA; Carol M. Highsmith, Inc.

Admission

State Bar Membership Required	Any state or U.S. District Court
Automatic Admission with State Bar Membership	No
Additional Test Required	No
Certificate of Good Standing Required	Yes
Sponsor Required	Yes, unless a member of U.S. District Court for the Eastern, Western or Southern District of New York
Oath Required	Yes, in person. In person not required if a member of the U.S. District Court for the Eastern, Western or Southern District of New York.
Fee	$150. $30 biennial registration fee.

Pro Hac Vice Admission

A Motion for Limited Admission *Pro Hac Vice* must be filed electronically by the sponsoring attorney along with a Petition, Affidavit of Sponsor, E-filing Registration Form, Certificate of Good Standing, and Proposed Order. $30 fee.

Address
U.S. District Court
445 Broadway, Room 509
Albany, NY 12207-2924

Telephone
518-257-1800
District Court Website
www.nynd.uscourts.gov
NDNY Federal Court Bar
www.ndnyfcba.org

Bankruptcy Court Admission

Regular: Any attorney who is admitted to practice before the District Court for the Northern District of New York is also admitted to practice before this court.

Pro Hac Vice: A member of the bar of any state or of any U.S. District Court not otherwise admitted to practice before the court may be permitted to practice on motion in this court only for a limited purpose in a particular case. An attorney seeking admission *pro hac vice* shall provide a certificate of good standing in support of counsel's motion for admission, as evidence of admission to the bar of any state or of any U.S. District Court, and shall pay to the District Court Clerk the $30 fee required to practice ex parte or on motion.

Bankruptcy Court Website
www.nynb.uscourts.gov

Telephone
518-257-1661

U.S. District Court – New York Southern District

Authorized Active Judges	Circuit
28	2

Admission

State Bar Membership Required	New York or a member of the U.S. District Court in Connecticut or Vermont and of the bar of the State in which such district court is located, provided such district court by its rule extends a corresponding privilege to members of the bar of this court
Automatic Admission with State Bar	No
Additional Test Required	No
Certificate of Good Standing Required	Yes, from **each** state where a member
Sponsor Required	Yes, in person for New York; Not in person for White Plains
Oath Required	Yes, before Judge in New York or Clerk in White Plains
Fee	$185

Pro Hac Vice Admission

An attorney may be admitted to practice in this Court in a single case through submission of a motion for admission *pro hac vice*. Applicants must be sponsored by an attorney who is admitted to practice before the bar of this Court (not admitted *pro hac vice*). Include:

(1) A check for $25

(2) A motion for admission *pro hac vice* with the applicant's full contact information and without a return date,

(3) An affidavit from the sponsoring attorney stating that he or she is in good standing with this Court and the applicant is of high moral character,

(4) Certificate(s) of Good Standing for the applicant from each of the states for which the applicant is a member of the bar, and which has been issued within 30 days,

(5) A proposed order for admission *pro hac vice*, and

(6) Proof of Service of the motion on all parties in the case.

Address
U.S. Courthouse
500 Pearl Street
New York, NY 10007

Telephone
212-805-0645
District Court Website
www.nysd.uscourts.gov

Bankruptcy Court Admission

Regular: An attorney who may practice in the U.S. District Court for the Southern District of New York may practice in this Court.

Pro Hac Vice: Upon motion, a member in good standing of the bar of any state or of any U.S. District Court may be permitted to practice in this Court in a particular case. $25 fee.

Bankruptcy Court Website
www.nysb.uscourts.gov

Telephone
212-668-2870

U.S. District Court – New York Western District

Authorized Active Judges	Circuit
4	2

Michael J. Dillon U.S. Courthouse. Photo: U.S. GSA by K.C. Kratt Photography

Admission

State Bar Membership Required	Any state if also a member of U.S. District Court in that state. If a member of the U.S. District Court for Southern, Eastern, or Northern District of New York, may be admitted to this Court without formal application upon filing a Certificate of Good Standing and fee.
Automatic Admission w/ State Bar	No
Additional Test Required	No
Cert of Good Standing Required	Yes, if a member of other New York U.S. District Court
Sponsor Required	Yes, if not member of other New York U.S. District Court
Oath Required	Yes
Fee	$200

Pro Hac Vice Admission

An attorney duly admitted to practice in any state, territory, district or foreign country may in the discretion of the Court be admitted *pro hac vice* to participate in any matter.
See Local Rules for local counsel requirements.

Address
U.S. District Court, Western District of New York
304 U.S. Courthouse, 68 Court Street
Buffalo, NY 14202-3498

Telephone
716-551-4211
District Court Website
www.nywd.uscourts.gov

Bankruptcy Court Admission

Regular: 1) A person admitted to the U.S. District Court for the Western District of New York before October 1, 1979, is admitted for bankruptcy practice in the Western District. 2) A person subsequently admitted to bankruptcy practice under prior local bankruptcy rules is admitted for bankruptcy practice in the Western District of New York. 3) Otherwise, a person admitted to practice before the U.S. District Court for the Western District of New York may apply by filing a petition.
Pro Hac Vice: An attorney duly admitted to practice in any state, territory, district, or foreign country may be admitted *pro hac vice* to participate in a bankruptcy case before the District or Bankruptcy Court under such terms or conditions as may be appropriate. No fee.

Bankruptcy Court Website
www.nywb.uscourts.gov

Telephone
585-613-4200

U.S. District Court – Vermont

Authorized Active Judges	Circuit
2	2

Admission

State Bar Membership Required	Vermont or any U.S. District Court within the First or Second Circuits
Automatic Admission with State Bar Membership	No
Additional Test Required	No
Certificate of Good Standing Required	No
Sponsor Required	Yes, in person
Oath Required	Yes, in person
Fee	$150, in person

Pro Hac Vice Admission

Any attorney who is a member of the Bar of any federal court or of the highest court of any state may apply for *pro hac vice* admission to this Court by fulfilling the following requirements: (1) motion from Sponsor, (2) Supporting Affidavit, and (3) $150 fee.

Address
U.S. District Court
Office of the Clerk
P.O. Box 945
Burlington, VT 05402-0945

Telephone
802-951-6301

District Court Website
www.vtd.uscourts.gov

Bankruptcy Court Admission

Regular: Members of the U.S. District Court of Vermont may practice before this Court.

Pro Hac Vice: Any attorney who is a member of the Bar of any federal court or of any state may apply for *pro hac vice* admission to this Court by submitting a motion from Sponsor and a Supporting Affidavit. Unless excused by the Court for good cause, an attorney admitted *pro hac vice* must remain at all times associated in the action with a member of the Bar of this Court upon whom all process, notices, and other papers must be served, who must sign all filings, and whose attendance is required at all hearings.

Bankruptcy Court Website
www.vtb.uscourts.gov

Telephone
802-776-2000

U.S. Court of Appeals for the Third Circuit

Authorized Active Judges	Circuit
14	3

James A. Byrne Federal Courthouse. Photos: U.S. Dist. Ct. Eastern Dist. Pennsylvania

Admission

Bar/Court Membership Required	Any state, another U.S. Court of Appeals, Supreme Court of the United States, or a U.S. District Court
Automatic Admission with State Bar Membership	No
Additional Test Required	No
Certificate of Good Standing Required	Yes
Sponsor Required	Yes
Oath Required	Yes
Fee	$190

Address
Office of the Clerk
U.S. Court of Appeals for the Third Circuit
21400 United States Courthouse
601 Market Street
Philadelphia, PA 19106-1790

Third Circuit Bar Association
www.thirdcircuitbar.org

Telephone
215-597-2995

Appeals Court Website
www.ca3.uscourts.gov

U.S. District Court – Delaware

Authorized Active Judges	Circuit
4	3

Admission

State Bar Membership Required	Delaware
Automatic Admission with State Bar Membership	No
Additional Test Required	No
Certificate of Good Standing Required	No
Sponsor Required	Yes, in person
Oath Required	Yes, in person
Fee	$165

Pro Hac Vice Admission

Attorneys admitted, practicing, and in good standing in another jurisdiction, who are not admitted to practice by the Supreme Court of the State of Delaware, may be admitted *pro hac vice* to the Bar of this Court in the discretion of the Court, such admission to be at the pleasure of the Court. Unless otherwise ordered by the Court, or authorized by the Constitution of the United States or acts of Congress, an applicant is not eligible for permission to practice *pro hac vice* if the applicant: (1) Resides in Delaware; or (2) Is regularly employed in Delaware; or (3) Is regularly engaged in business, professional, or other similar activities in Delaware. $25 fee.
Association with Delaware counsel required. An attorney not admitted to practice by the Supreme Court of the State of Delaware may not be admitted *pro hac vice* in this Court unless associated with an attorney who is a member of the Bar of this Court and who maintains an office in the District of Delaware for the regular transaction of business.

Address
Clerk, U. S. District Court
844 N. King Street
Room 4209, Unit 18
Wilmington, DE 19801

Telephone
302-573-6170

District Court Website
www.ded.uscourts.gov

Bankruptcy Court Admission

Regular: The Bar of this Court shall consist of those persons heretofore admitted to practice in the District Court.
Pro Hac Vice: See District Court *pro hac vice* rules above. $25 fee per calendar year.

Bankruptcy Court Website
www.deb.uscourts.gov

Telephone
302-252-2900

U.S. District Court – New Jersey

Authorized Active Judges	Circuit
17	3

Martin Luther King Federal Building & Courthouse. Photo: U.S. GSA

Admission

State Bar Membership Required	New Jersey
Automatic Admission with State Bar Membership	No
Additional Test Required	No
Certificate of Good Standing Required	No
Sponsor Required	No
Oath Required	By attorney, judge or notary of any jurisdiction
Fee	$200

Pro Hac Vice Admission

Local counsel must file papers, enter appearance for parties, sign stipulations or sign and receive payments on judgments, decrees or orders
Payment of $150 on each admission payable to the Clerk, U.S. District Court and any requisite payments to New Jersey Lawyers' Fund for Client Protection (call 609-292-8079).

Address
U.S. District Court of New Jersey
50 Walnut Street, Room 4015
Newark, NJ 07101
Attn: Attorney Admissions

Telephone
973-622-4810
District Court Website
www.njd.uscourts.gov
Historical Society U.S. DCDNJ
www.history.njd.uscourts.gov

Bankruptcy Court Admission

Regular: The bar of this Court shall consist of any attorney admitted to practice before the U.S. District Court for the District of New Jersey.
Pro Hac Vice: Attorneys may seek admission *pro hac vice* by application on 7 days notice to the debtor, any committee, the United States Trustee, and any other party as the Court may direct. The application must be accompanied by this Court's form order for admission *pro hac vice*. $150 fee and $208 payable to Fund for Client Protection.

Bankruptcy Court Website
www.njb.uscourts.gov

Telephone
973-645-4764

U.S. District Court – Pennsylvania Eastern District

Authorized Active Judges	Circuit
22	3

James A. Byrne Federal Courthouse. Photos: U.S. Dist. Ct. Eastern Dist. Pennsylvania

Admission

Commonwealth Bar Membership Required	Pennsylvania
Automatic Admission with Commonwealth Bar Membership	No
Additional Test Required	No
Certificate of Good Standing Required	No
Sponsor Required	Yes
Oath Required	Yes
Fee	$175

Pro Hac Vice Admission

Attorneys admitted in another state or federal court may submit the prescribed form, sponsor's motion and $40 fee.

Address
U.S. District Court, Eastern District of Pennsylvania
U.S. Courthouse
601 Market Street, Room 2609
Philadelphia, PA 19106-1797

Telephone
215-597-7704
District Court Website
www.paed.uscourts.gov
Historical Society of the U.S. DCEDP
www.paed.uscourts.gov/us21000.asp#HistSocApp

Bankruptcy Court Admission

Regular: An attorney who is admitted to practice in the U.S. District Court for the Eastern District of Pennsylvania and presently in good standing before the district court is automatically admitted to practice before this court and is a member of the bar of this court.
Pro Hac Vice: An attorney who is a member in good standing of the bar of any U.S. District Court or the highest court of any state or of the District of Columbia may be admitted to practice before this court in a particular case. [Rules vary for adversary proceedings versus non-adversary proceedings]. $40 fee.

Bankruptcy Court Website
www.paeb.uscourts.gov

Telephone
215-408-2800

U.S. District Court – Pennsylvania Middle District

Authorized Active Judges	Circuit
6	3

William J. Nealon Federal Building & U.S. Courthouse. Photos: U.S. GSA by Carol M. Highsmith, Inc.

Admission

Commonwealth Bar Membership Required	Pennsylvania
Automatic Admission with Commonwealth Bar	No
Additional Test Required	No
Certificate of Good Standing Required	No
Sponsor Required	Yes, in person
Oath Required	Yes, including Code of Prof. Conduct
Fee	$175

Pro Hac Vice Admission

An attorney, who is admitted to practice in any U.S. District Court and any state, may be admitted to practice by leave granted in the discretion of the court for a particular case.

Address
William J. Nealon Federal Building & U.S. Courthouse
235 N. Washington Ave., P.O. Box 1148
Scranton, PA 18501

Telephone
570-207-5600
District Court Website
www.pamd.uscourts.gov

Bankruptcy Court Admission

Regular: Except for *pro ha vice* admissions, no attorney may appear on behalf of another unless first admitted to practice in the U.S. District Court for the Middle District of Pennsylvania.

Pro Hac Vice: An attorney who is admitted to practice before any U.S. District Court and any state or the District of Columbia and who is in good standing in every jurisdiction where admitted to practice, and who is not subject to pending disciplinary proceedings in any jurisdiction, may be admitted to practice before this court, but only for the purpose of a particular case. A request for admission must be made by written motion of a member of the bar of this court or by the attorney intending to practice before this court. The court in its discretion may grant an oral motion for admission made in open court. No fee.

Bankruptcy Court Website
www.pamb.uscourts.gov

Telephone
717-901-2800

U.S. District Court – Pennsylvania Western District

Authorized Active Judges	Circuit
10	3

U.S. Post Office and Courthouse. Photos: LC- DIG-pplot-13727-01458; LC-DIG-pplot-13727-01453

Admission

Commonwealth Membership Required	Pennsylvania, Supreme Court of the United States or any U.S. District Court
Automatic Admission with Commonwealth Bar Membership	No
Additional Test Required	No
Certificate of Good Standing Required	No
Sponsor Required	Yes, oral motion required
Oath Required	Yes
Fee	$160

Pro Hac Vice Admission

All motions for admission *pro hac vice* must be submitted by a member of the bar of this Court on behalf of the attorney to be admitted *pro hac vice* with $40 filing fee.

Address
U.S. District Court, Western District of Pennsylvania
U.S. Post Office & Courthouse, Room 3100
Pittsburgh, PA 15219

Telephone
412-208-7500
District Court Website
www.pawd.uscourts.gov

Bankruptcy Court Admission

Regular: Attorneys who are admitted to the bar of the U.S. District Court for the Western District of Pennsylvania are admitted to the bar of this Court.

Pro Hac Vice. No one, other than an attorney regularly admitted to practice in this Court, shall appear in any proceeding on behalf of any trustee, creditor, or other party in interest, except upon motion filed with the Clerk and order entered by the Court. Every motion to be admitted *pro hac vice* must be filed by an attorney admitted to practice in this District. If a motion for *pro hac vice* is made in open Court, it shall be followed by a written motion signed by local counsel and the applicant. The Court may require counsel to provide evidence of admission in another district. $40 fee.

Bankruptcy Court Website
www.pawb.uscourts.gov

Telephone
412-644-4060

U.S. District Court – U.S. Virgin Islands

Circuit
3

Photos: U.S. GSA; U.S. DOJ

Admission

Territory Bar Membership Required	Virgin Islands
Automatic Admission with Territory Bar	No
Additional Test Required	No
Certificate of Good Standing Required	No
Sponsor Required	Yes, in person
Oath Required	Yes, in person
Fee	None currently, fees being considered

Pro Hac Vice Admission

Any member of the bar of any court of the U.S. or of any state, who is not under suspension or disbarment by any court and is ineligible for admission to the bar of the Court, may in the discretion of the Court, on motion, be permitted to participate in a particular case. $250 fee.
An appearance as counsel of record shall be filed promptly by a member of the bar of the Court (local counsel) upon whom all notices, orders and pleadings may be served.
May be admitted *pro hac vice* in no more than a total of 3 cases in any calendar year.
The court has special admission rules for patent attorneys.

Address
Office of the Clerk
Almeric L. Christian Federal Building
3013 Estate Golden Rock, Room 219
St. Croix, VI 00820

Telephone
340-718-1130

District Court Website
www.vid.uscourts.gov

Bankruptcy Court Admission

Regular: Attorneys who are admitted to the bar of the U.S. District Court for the Virgin Islands are admitted to the bar of this Court.
Pro Hac Vice: Motion to be admitted *pro hac vice* shall be filed by an attorney admitted in this district. If a motion for *pro hac vice* is made orally in open court, it shall be followed by the filing of a written motion. The Court may require counsel to provide evidence of admission in another district. An attorney not admitted to practice in the Virgin Islands may not be admitted *pro hac vice* in this Court unless associated with an attorney who is a member of the Bar of this Court and who maintains an office in this district for the regular transaction of business, upon whom all filings in the case shall be served and who shall be required to sign all papers filed with the Clerk. Association with local counsel shall not be required for the filing or prosecution of a proof of claim or response to an objection to a proof of claim. The Court may, however, direct counsel to associate with local counsel if the claim litigation will involve extensive discovery or trial time. $250 fee.

Bankruptcy Court Website
See District Court website

Telephone
340-774-8310

U.S. Court of Appeals for the Fourth Circuit

Authorized Active Judges	Circuit
15	4

Lewis F. Powell, Jr. U.S. Courthouse. Photo: U.S. GSA by Brandon Webster Photography

Admission

Bar/Court Membership Required	Any state or federal
Additional Test Required	No
Certificate of Good Standing Required	No
Sponsor Required	Yes
Oath Required	Yes
Fee	$170

Address
Office of the Clerk
U.S. Court of Appeals for the Fourth Circuit
1100 E. Main Street, Suite 501
Richmond, VA 23219-3517

Telephone
804-916-2700

Appeals Court Website
www.ca4.uscourts.gov

U.S. District Court – Maryland

Authorized Active Judges	Circuit
10	4

Edward A. Garmatz Federal Building & U.S. Courthouse. Photos: U.S. GSA by Carol M. Highsmith, Inc.

Admission

State Bar Membership Required	1) Members of the Maryland Bar, or 2) Non-Maryland Attorneys licensed in any other State or DC. Note: If the attorney is a member of the U.S. District Court where he/she resides and said Court does not offer reciprocity to members of the Maryland Bar with offices in Maryland, they cannot apply. 3) Attorneys not admitted to the Maryland Bar, who maintain a law office in Maryland, may not apply.
Automatic Admission with State Bar Membership	No
Additional Test Required	No
Cert of Good Standing Required	No
Sponsor Required	Yes, in person
Oath Required	Yes
Fee	$175. Renew every 6 years for $60.

Pro Hac Vice Admission

The Court may permit an attorney (except a member of the Maryland Bar or an attorney maintaining a law office in Maryland) who is a member of the Bar of any other U.S. Court or any state to appear and participate as counsel in a particular civil case. $50 fee.
Any party represented by an attorney who has been admitted *pro hac vice* must also be represented by an attorney who has been formally admitted to the Bar of this Court.
To be admitted *pro hac vice*, a member of the Bar of this Court must move the admission.

Address
U.S. District Court
101 West Lombard Street, 4th Floor
Baltimore, MD 21201

Telephone
410-962-2600
District Court Website
www.mdd.uscourts.gov

Bankruptcy Court Admission

Regular: Only members of the U.S. District Court of Maryland may appear as counsel.
Pro Hac Vice: The court can permit any attorney (except a member of the Maryland Bar) who is a member of the Bar of any other U.S. Court or any state to participate as counsel in a particular bankruptcy case. $50 fee.

Bankruptcy Court Website
www.mdb.uscourts.gov

Telephone
410-962-2688

Bankruptcy Bar Assn Dist. of Maryland
www.bankruptcybar.org

U.S. District Court – North Carolina Eastern District

Authorized Active Judges	Circuit
4	4

Terry Sanford Federal Building & Courthouse. Photo: U.S. Dist. Ct. North Carolina Eastern Dist.

Admission

State Bar Membership Required	North Carolina
Automatic Admission with State Bar Membership	No
Additional Test Required	No
Certificate of Good Standing Required	No, unless admitted to U.S. District Court for the Middle or Western Districts of North Carolina
Sponsor Required	Yes (2), unless admitted to U.S. District Court for the Middle or Western Districts of North Carolina
Oath Required	Yes, in person if not admitted to U.S. District Court for the Middle or Western Districts of North Carolina
Fee	$180

Pro Hac Vice Admission

Attorneys who are members in good standing of the bar of a U.S. District Court and the bar of the highest court of any state or the District of Columbia may practice in this court for a particular case in association with a member of the bar of this court.

Address
U.S. District Court
Eastern District of North Carolina
Office of the Clerk
P.O. Box 25670
Raleigh, NC 27611

Telephone
919-645-1700

District Court Website
www.nced.uscourts.gov

Bankruptcy Court Admission

Regular: Only those persons who are admitted to the bar of the U.S. District Court for the Eastern District of North Carolina are admitted to practice before this court.

Pro Hac Vice: Attorneys who are members of the bar of a U.S. District Court and the bar of the highest court of any state or the District of Columbia may practice in this court for a particular case in association with a member of the bar of this court. No fee.

Bankruptcy Court Website
www.nceb.uscourts.gov

Telephone
252-237-0248

U.S. District Court – North Carolina Middle District

Authorized Active Judges	Circuit
4	4

L. R. Preyer Federal Building-Post Office-Courthouse. Photo: U.S. Dist. Ct. North Carolina Middle Dist.

Admission

State Bar Membership Required	North Carolina
Automatic Admission with State Bar	No
Additional Test Required	No
Certificate of Good Standing Required	No, unless admitted to U.S. District Court for the Eastern or Western Districts of North Carolina
Sponsor Required	Yes, unless admitted to U.S. District Court for the Eastern or Western Districts of North Carolina
Oath Required	Yes, in person if not admitted to U.S. District Court for the Eastern or Western Dist. of North Carolina
Fee	$150

Pro Hac Vice Admission

Attorneys who are members in good standing of the bar of the highest court of any state or the District of Columbia may practice in this court for a particular case in association with a member of the bar of this court.

Address
U.S. District Court
324 W. Market Street
Greensboro, NC 27401
Attn: Attorney Admissions Clerk

Telephone
336-332-6000

District Court Website
www.ncmd.uscourts.gov

Bankruptcy Court Admission

Regular: Only those persons who are admitted to practice before the U.S. District Court for the Middle District of North Carolina are allowed to practice before the Bankruptcy Court.

Pro Hac Vice: Any attorney who is a member of the bar of any District Court of the U.S. other than the Middle Dist. of North Carolina, may, in the discretion of the Bankruptcy Court, appear and participate *pro hac vice* in any case without general admission before this Bankruptcy Court if it is not abused by frequent appearances, there is a written motion filed meeting all the requirements and such attorney appears with local counsel admitted to the U.S. District Court for the Middle District of North Carolina No fee.

Bankruptcy Court Website
www.ncmb.uscourts.gov

Telephone
336-358-4000

U.S. District Court – North Carolina Western District

Authorized Active Judges	Circuit
5	4

Charles R. Jonas Federal Building. Photo: U.S. Dist. Ct., North Carolina Western Dist.

Admission

State Bar Membership Required	North Carolina
Automatic Admission with State Bar Membership	No
Additional Test Required	No
Certificate of Good Standing Required	No, unless admitted to U.S. District Court for the Eastern or Middle Districts of North Carolina
Sponsor Required	Yes, unless admitted to U.S. District Court for Eastern or Middle Districts of North Carolina
Oath Required	Yes, in person if not admitted to U.S. District Court for the Eastern or Middle Districts of North Carolina
Fee	$250

Pro Hac Vice Admission

Special, *pro hac vice* and nunc pro tunc admissions are discretionary and additional requirements or expectations for such admissions may be found in the Standing Civil Order of the judge to whom the case is assigned.
The motion shall be filed electronically by local counsel who must be registered to file electronically. The motion shall include the e-mail address of the attorney seeking admission; and shall be accompanied by the $250 fee (for each special admission).

Address
U.S. District Court
401 W. Trade Street, Rm. 210
Charlotte, NC 28202

Telephone
704-350-7416
District Court Website
www.ncwd.uscourts.gov

Bankruptcy Court Admission

Regular: Attorneys admitted to the U.S. District Court for the Western District of North Carolina are members of this Court.
Pro Hac Vice: Any lawyer who is a member of the Bar of the Supreme Court of the United States or any state, may, in the discretion of the judges of this Court, be permitted to appear in a particular case. The Court encourages out-of-state attorneys to associate a member of the bar of this Court in all cases, but will not require such association where the amount in controversy or the importance of the case does not appear to justify double employment of counsel. Special admission will be the exception and not the rule, and no out-of-state counsel will be permitted to practice frequently or regularly in this Court without the association of local counsel. $250 fee.

Bankruptcy Court Website
www.ncwb.uscourts.gov

Telephone
704-350-7500

U.S. District Court – South Carolina

Authorized Active Judges	Circuit
10	4

Strom Thurmond Federal Building & U.S. Courthouse. Photos: LC-DIG-pplot-13826-01835; LC-DIG-pplot-13826-01844

Admission

State Bar Membership Required	South Carolina
Automatic Admission with State Bar Membership	No
Additional Test Required	No, but see requirement for trial experience under Rule 403(b) of the South Carolina Appellate Court Rules or equivalent judicial clerkship experience
Certificate of Good Standing Required	No
Sponsor Required	Yes (2)
Oath Required	Yes
Fee	$150

Pro Hac Vice Admission

Upon motion of an attorney admitted to practice before this Court, any person who is a member of the Bar of a U.S. District Court and the Bar of any State or the District of Columbia shall be permitted to appear in a particular matter in association with a member of the Bar of this Court. See motion and local counsel requirements.

Address
USDC Attorney Admissions
901 Richland Street
Columbia, SC 29201

Telephone
803-765-5789
District Court Website
www.scd.uscourts.gov

Bankruptcy Court Admission

Regular: An attorney who is admitted to practice in the United States District Court for the District of South Carolina is admitted to practice in this Court.
Pro Hac Vice: See District Court rules above. $250 fee.

Bankruptcy Court Website
www.scb.uscourts.gov

Telephone
803-765-5436

U.S. District Court – Virginia Eastern District

Authorized Active Judges	Circuit
11	4

Walter E. Hoffman U.S. Courthouse. Photo: U.S. Dist. Ct. Virginia Eastern Dist.

Admission

Commonwealth Bar Membership Required	Virginia. Also, any attorney admitted to practice in the Western District of Virginia shall be permitted to practice in the Eastern District of Virginia upon filing a Certificate of Good Standing from the Western Dist. of Virginia.
Auto Admission with Commonwealth Bar	No
Additional Test Required	No
Certificate of Good Standing Required	Copy of Virginia Bar Card
Sponsor Required	Yes (2)
Oath Required	Yes, in person
Fee	$150

Pro Hac Vice Admission

Upon written motion by a member of this Court, a practitioner qualified to practice in the U.S. District Court of another state or the District of Columbia may appear for specific cases *pro hac vice* before this Court including oral arguments of motions and trial provided:

(a) The rules of the U.S. District Court of the district in which the practitioner maintains an office extend a similar privilege to members of the bar of this Court; and

(b) That such practitioners from another state or the District of Columbia shall be accompanied by a member of the bar of this Court in all appearances before this Court.

Address
U.S. District Court, Eastern District of Virginia
600 Granby Street, Room 193-B
Norfolk, VA 23510

Telephone
757-222-7201
District Court Website
www.vaed.uscourts.gov

Bankruptcy Court Admission

Regular: Attorneys admitted to practice before this Court shall comprise the Bar of the U.S. Bankruptcy Court for the Eastern Dist. of Virginia. To qualify for admission and maintain the right to practice before this Court, must take an oath and remain a member of the Bar of Virginia and file a written application endorsed by 2 qualified members of this Court. Any attorney who is a member of the Bar of the U.S. Bankruptcy Court for the Western Dist. of Virginia shall be permitted to practice in the courts of the Eastern Dist. of Virginia upon filing a Certificate from the U.S. Bankruptcy Court for Western Dist. of Virginia stating the attorney is a member.

Pro Hac Vice: If admitted in another state, submit application & Sponsor motion. No fee.

Bankruptcy Court Website
www.vaeb.uscourts.gov

Telephone
804-916-2400

Bankruptcy Bar Assn Northern Virginia
www.nvbba.org

U.S. District Court – Virginia Western District

Authorized Active Judges	Circuit
4	4

Richard H. Poff U.S. Courthouse. Photo: U.S. DOJ

Admission

Commonwealth Bar Membership Required	Virginia. Also, any attorney admitted to the U.S. District Court for the Eastern District of Virginia is permitted to practice in this Court upon filing a Certificate of Good Standing from the Eastern District of Virginia.
Automatic Admission with Commonwealth Bar Membership	No
Additional Test Required	No
Cert. of Good Standing Required	No
Sponsor Required	Yes (2)
Oath Required	Yes
Fee	$150

Pro Hac Vice Admission

Attorneys who are not qualified and licensed to practice under the laws of Virginia, but who are licensed to the practice before the Supreme Court of the United States, or before any state or the District of Columbia, may appear only in association with a member of the bar of this Court, upon motion of such member, and only for the conduct of a case in which he or she is associated.

Address
U.S. District Court
210 Franklin Road, Room 308
Roanoke, VA 24011

Telephone
540-857-5100
District Court Website
www.vawd.uscourts.gov

Bankruptcy Court Admission

Regular: Those attorneys who are admitted to practice before this Court shall comprise the Bar of the U.S. Bankruptcy Court for the Western District of Virginia.
File written application accompanied by an endorsement by a qualified member this Court stating that the applicant is of good moral character and professional reputation and is qualified to practice bankruptcy law. An oath must be administered by the Court.
Any attorney who is a member of the Virginia State Bar and the Bar of the U.S. Bankruptcy Court for the Eastern District of Virginia shall be permitted to practice in the Bankruptcy Court for the Western District of Virginia upon filing a Certificate from the Clerk of the U.S. Bankruptcy Court for the Eastern District of Virginia stating the attorney is a member.
Pro Hac Vice: Attorneys who are not qualified and licensed to practice under the laws of Virginia, but who are members of the U.S. Supreme Court, any state or District of Columbia, may appear on a *pro hac vice* basis only in association with a member of this Court. No fee.

Bankruptcy Court Website
www.vawb.uscourts.gov

Telephone
540-857-2391

U.S. District Court – West Virginia Northern District

Authorized Active Judges	Circuit
3	4

Admission

State Bar Membership Required	West Virginia
Automatic Admission with State Bar Membership	No
Additional Test Required	No
Certificate of Good Standing Required	No
Sponsor Required	Yes
Oath Required	Yes
Fee	$150

Pro Hac Vice Admission

If not a member of West Virginia bar, may submit a verified statement of application listing (1) the proceeding before the court, (2) where admitted, (3) member of West Virginia bar who will be responsible local attorney, (4) all matters before West Virginia tribunals in which said person has been involved in preceding 24 months, unless such person is admitted to practice in West Virginia, (5) all matters before West Virginia tribunals or bodies in which any member of applicant's firm, partnership, corporation or other operating entity is or has been involved in the preceding 24 months, unless such person is admitted to practice in West Virginia, (6) a representation by the applicant for each state, the District of Columbia or any other country where said applicant has been admitted to practice, stating that the applicant is in good standing with the bar of every such jurisdiction and that he or she has not been disciplined in any such jurisdiction within the preceding 24 months, and (7) an agreement to comply with all laws, rules and regulations of West Virginia state and local governments, where applicable, including taxing authorities and any standard for pro bono civil and criminal indigent defense legal services; and upon payment of $50 fee.

Address

Clerk, U.S. District Court
P.O. Box 471
1125 Chapline Street, Suite 1000
Wheeling, WV 26003

Telephone

304-232-0011

District Court Website

www.wvnd.uscourts.gov

Bankruptcy Court Admission

Follows District Court rules above. No fee for *pro hac vice* admission.

Bankruptcy Court Website

www.wvnb.uscourts.gov

Telephone

304-233-1655

U.S. District Court – West Virginia Southern District

Authorized Active Judges	Circuit
5	4

Admission

State Bar Membership Required	West Virginia
Automatic Admission with State Bar Membership	No
Additional Test Required	No
Certificate of Good Standing Required	No
Sponsor Required	Yes
Oath Required	Yes
Fee	$150

Pro Hac Vice Admission

Must be admitted in another state. The Sponsoring Attorney must be a member of the bar of this court, have an office for the practice of law in West Virginia, and practice law primarily in West Virginia. $50 fee per appearance.

Address
Clerk, U.S. District Court
Robert C. Byrd United States Courthouse
300 Virginia Street East, Room 2400
Charleston, WV 25301

Telephone
304-347-3000

District Court Website
www.wvsd.uscourts.gov

Bankruptcy Court Admission

Regular: Attorneys admitted to practice in the U.S. District Court for the Southern District of West Virginia are automatically admitted to practice before this Court.

Pro Hac Vice: Any visiting attorney, not admitted to practice before the U. S. District Court, S.D.W.V., who is a member in good standing of the bar of the Supreme Court of the United States, or of the bar of the highest court of any state in the United States, or of the bar of the District of Columbia, may file a motion *pro hac vice* with the Bankruptcy Court. Such motion shall contain a statement identifying by exact name and address the bar of which the visiting attorney is a member in good standing and will ordinarily be granted in matters of disputed claims litigation and enforcement of Bankruptcy Court judgments, but, otherwise, it shall be granted only on a case-by-case basis for cause. If no order is entered admitting an attorney *pro hac vice*, a visiting attorney must associate with local counsel admitted to practice before the Court, who shall endorse all pleadings filed with the Court and accompany the visiting attorney upon the visiting attorney's initial appearance before the Court. thereafter, the local counsel may, by and with the consent of the Court, be excused from further attendance during the proceedings, and the visiting attorney may be permitted to continue to appear for the purpose of the particular case. $50 fee.

Bankruptcy Court Website
www.wvsb.uscourts.gov

Telephone
304-347-3003

U.S. Court of Appeals for the Fifth Circuit

Authorized Active Judges	Circuit
17	5

John Minor Wisdom Court of Appeals Building. Photo: LC-DIG-pplot-13820-01716

Admission

Bar/Court Membership Required	Any state, another U.S. Court of Appeals, Supreme Court of United States, or U.S. District Court
Additional Test Required	No
Certificate of Good Standing Required	Yes
Sponsor Required	Yes
Oath Required	Yes
Fee	$200

Address
Office of the Clerk
U.S. Court of Appeals for the Fifth Circuit
600 S. Maestri Place
New Orleans, LA 70130

Telephone
504-310-7700

Appeals Court Website
www.ca5.uscourts.gov

U.S. District Court – Louisiana Eastern District

Authorized Active Judges	Circuit
12	5

Hale Boggs Federal Building. Photo: U.S. DOJ

Admission

State Bar Membership Required	Louisiana
Automatic Admission with State Bar Membership	No
Additional Test Required	No
Certificate of Good Standing Required	No, unless *pro hac vice* admission
Sponsor Required	Yes (2)
Oath Required	Yes, in person unless exempted
Fee	$150. $5 annual fee paid triennially.

Pro Hac Vice Admission

Any member in good standing of the bar of any court of the United States or of any state and who is ineligible to become a member of the bar of this court, may, upon written motion of counsel of record who is a member of the bar of this court, by ex parte order, be permitted to appear and participate as co-counsel in a particular case.
The motion must have attached to it a certificate by the presiding judge or clerk of the state, or court of the United States, where he or she has been so admitted to practice, showing that the applicant attorney has been so admitted in such court, and that he or she is in good standing therein.
Local counsel shall be responsible to the court at all stages of the proceedings.

Address
U.S. District Court, Eastern District of Louisiana
500 Poydras Street
New Orleans, LA 70130

Telephone
504-589-7650

District Court Website
www.laed.uscourts.gov

Bankruptcy Court Admission

Regular: Every member in good standing of the bar of the U.S. District Court for the Eastern District of Louisiana is entitled to practice before this court.
Pro Hac Vice: Any member of the bar of any court of the United States or any state may be permitted to participate in a case upon written motion. The motion must have attached to it a certificate by the presiding judge or clerk of the highest court of the state, or court of the United States, where the applicant has been admitted to practice showing that the applicant attorney has been admitted and is in good standing. The applicant attorney must state under oath whether any disciplinary proceedings or criminal charges have been instituted against him/her and, if so, must disclose full information about the proceedings or charges and the results. Unless otherwise ordered by the court, it is not necessary for any attorney entitled to practice before the court or permitted to appear and participate in a case or proceeding to associate with or to designate an attorney with an office in this district upon whom notices, rulings, and communications may be served. No fee.

Bankruptcy Court Website
www.laeb.uscourts.gov

Telephone
504-589-7878

U.S. District Court – Louisiana Middle District

Authorized Active Judges	Circuit
3	5

Russell B. Long Federal Building. Photo: U.S. Dist. Ct. Louisiana Middle Dist.

Admission

State Bar Membership Required	Louisiana
Automatic Admission with State Bar Membership	No
Additional Test Required	No
Certificate of Good Standing Required	Yes
Sponsor Required	Yes (2)
Oath Required	Yes
Fee	$180. $45 fee paid triennially.

Pro Hac Vice Admission

Any member of the bar of any court of the United States or any state and who is ineligible to become a member of the bar of this court, may, upon written motion of counsel of record who is a member of the bar of this court, by ex parte order, be permitted to appear and participate as co-counsel in a particular case.
Motion must have attached a Certificate of Good Standing from court where admitted.

Address
Clerk, U.S. District Court
Attn: Attorney Admissions
777 Florida Street Suite
139 Baton Rouge, LA 70801

Telephone
225-389-3500

District Court Website
www.lamd.uscourts.gov

Bankruptcy Court Admission

Regular: Attorneys admitted to practice before the U.S. District Court for the Middle District of Louisiana may represent persons in this court.
Pro Hac Vice: An attorney ineligible for admission to the bar of the U.S. District Court for the Middle District of Louisiana, who is a member in good standing of the bar of any United States Court or the highest court of any State, Territory or Insular Possession of the United States, and of good moral character may be permitted to appear and participate in a specific case or proceeding, upon ex parte motion. Permission to appear *pro hac vice* in the bankruptcy court does not constitute permission to appear in the district court. Except as authorized by the United States Constitution, Act of Congress or court order, an applicant is not eligible to practice *pro hac vice* if the applicant: (1) resides in Louisiana; (2) is regularly employed in Louisiana; or (3) is regularly engaged in business or professional activities in Louisiana. Certificate of Good Standing required. No fee.

Bankruptcy Court Website
www.lamb.uscourts.gov

Telephone
225-389-0211

U.S. District Court – Louisiana Western District

Authorized Active Judges	Circuit
7	5

Admission

State Bar Membership Required	Louisiana
Automatic Admission with State Bar Membership	No
Additional Test Required	No
Certificate of Good Standing Required	Yes
Sponsor Required	Yes (2)
Oath Required	Yes
Fee	$175

Pro Hac Vice Admission

Any member in good standing of the bar of any court of the United States or of the highest court of any state and who is ineligible to become a member of the bar of this court, may, upon written motion of counsel of record who is a member of the bar of this court, by ex parte order, be permitted to appear and participate as co-counsel in a particular case.
The motion must have attached to it a certificate by the presiding judge or clerk of the highest court of the state, or court of the United States, where he or she has been so admitted to practice, showing that the applicant attorney has been so admitted in such court, and that he or she is in good standing therein.

Address

Clerk, United States District Court
300 Fannin Street, Suite 1167
Shreveport, LA 71101

Telephone

318-676-4228

District Court Website

www.lawd.uscourts.gov

Bankruptcy Court Admission

Regular: All attorneys appearing in Bankruptcy Court for the Western District of Louisiana must be admitted to practice in the Western District of Louisiana.
Pro Hac Vice: See District Court rules above. $25 fee.

Bankruptcy Court Website

www.lawb.uscourts.gov

Telephone

318-676-4267

U.S. District Court – Mississippi Northern District

Authorized Active Judges	Circuit
3	5

Admission

State Bar Membership Required	Mississippi
Automatic Admission with State Bar Membership	No
Additional Test Required	No
Certificate of Good Standing Required	Certificate of Admission to Practice
Sponsor Required	Yes
Oath Required	Yes, in person
Fee	$160

Pro Hac Vice Admission

A "non-resident attorney" is a person not admitted to practice law in this state but who is admitted in another state or territory of the United States or of the District of Columbia and is not disbarred or suspended from practice in any jurisdiction. $100 fee per case.

A non-resident attorney is eligible for admission *pro hac vice* if that lawyer:
1) lawfully practices solely on behalf of the lawyer's client and its commonly owned organizational affiliates, regardless of where the lawyer resides or works; or
2) neither resides nor is regularly employed at an office in this state; or
3) resides in this state but (a) lawfully practices from offices in one or more other states and (b) practices no more than temporarily in this state, whether by admission *pro hac vice* or in other lawful ways; or
4) is a government attorney employed on a full time basis and is lawfully admitted to practice in another jurisdiction.

Address
Clerk, U.S. District Court
Northern District of Mississippi
911 Jackson Avenue, Room 369
Oxford, MS 38655

Telephone
662-234-1971

District Court Website
www.msnd.uscourts.gov

Bankruptcy Court Admission

Regular: Follows District Court rules.

Pro Hac Vice: A non-resident attorney who is not a member of the Mississippi Bar and is not authorized to practice before the Mississippi Supreme Court and is not admitted to practice in the United States District Courts for the Northern or Southern Districts of Mississippi may apply to be admitted *pro hac vice* by comity to practice in a particular civil action in the court upon compliance with the rules. No fee.

Bankruptcy Court Website
www.msnb.uscourts.gov

Telephone
662-369-2596

U.S. District Court – Mississippi Southern District

Authorized Active Judges	Circuit
6	5

James O. Eastland U.S. Courthouse. Photo: National Archives, RG 121-BS, Box 51, Jackson Folder, Print 8153

Admission

State Bar Membership Required	Mississippi
Automatic Admission with State Bar Membership	No
Additional Test Required	No
Certificate of Good Standing Required	Cert. of Admission to Practice
Sponsor Required	Yes
Oath Required	Yes
Fee	$160

Pro Hac Vice Admission

A "non-resident attorney" is a person not admitted to practice law in this state but who is admitted in another state or territory of the United States or of the District of Columbia and is not disbarred or suspended from practice in any jurisdiction. $100 fee per case.

A non-resident attorney is eligible for admission *pro hac vice* if that lawyer:
5) lawfully practices solely on behalf of the lawyer's client and its commonly owned organizational affiliates, regardless of where the lawyer resides or works; or
6) neither resides nor is regularly employed at an office in this state; or
7) resides in this state but (a) lawfully practices from offices in one or more other states and (b) practices no more than temporarily in this state, whether by admission *pro hac vice* or in other lawful ways; or
8) is a government attorney employed on a full time basis and is lawfully admitted to practice in another jurisdiction.

Address

Clerk, U.S. District Court
James O. Eastland United States Courthouse
245 East Capitol Street, Room 316
Jackson, MS 39201-2409

Telephone

601-965-4439

District Court Website

www.mssd.uscourts.gov

Bankruptcy Court Admission

Regular: Follows District Court rules.

Pro Hac Vice: A non-resident attorney who is not a member of the Mississippi Bar and is not authorized to practice before the Mississippi Supreme Court and is not admitted to practice in the U.S. District Courts for the Northern or Southern Districts of Mississippi may apply to be admitted *pro hac vice* in a particular civil action in the court upon compliance with the rules. No fee.

Bankruptcy Court Website

www.mssb.uscourts.gov

Telephone

601-965-5301

U.S. District Court – Texas Eastern District

Authorized Active Judges	Circuit
8	5

Admission

State Bar Membership Required	Any state or federal
Automatic Admission with State Bar Membership	No
Additional Test Required	No
Certificate of Good Standing Required	No
Sponsor Required	Yes, from member of State Bar of Texas or a U.S. District Court
Oath Required	Yes
Fee	$150. $10 triennial fee is currently waived.

Pro Hac Vice Admission

An attorney who is not admitted to practice before this court may represent a party in any case in this court only upon an approved application to appear *pro hac vice*.
Such application also shall be accompanied by a $100 fee.

Address
Clerk, U.S. District Court
ATTN: Attorney Admissions Clerk
300 Willow Street, Room 104
Beaumont, TX 77701

Telephone
409-654-7000

District Court Website
www.txed.uscourts.gov

Bankruptcy Court Admission

Regular: The District Court Rules govern attorney admission.
Pro Hac Vice: A request for temporary admittance when an attorney is not admitted to practice in the Eastern District of Texas is generally governed by the Eastern District Court Rules except that: 1) the Court will rule upon the application and the applicant must attach a separate proposed order to the request; 2) the prescribed admission fee is waived if the attorney has not previously asked for temporary admittance within one year of the request; 3) the applicant must list, by case style, case number and application filing date, all other pro hac vice applications granted in the Bankruptcy Court within the year preceding the application.
Attorneys frequently appearing before the Bankruptcy Court must seek admission to the Eastern District of Texas pursuant to the Eastern District Court Rules. Unless otherwise authorized by the Court, an attorney may not be admitted to practice before the Bankruptcy Court on a *pro hac vice* basis on more than 3 occasions in any given 12-month period.

Bankruptcy Court Website
www.txeb.uscourts.gov

Telephone
903-590-3200

U.S. District Court – Texas Northern District

Authorized Active Judges	Circuit
12	5

Admission

State Bar Membership Required	Any state or District of Columbia
Automatic Admission with State Bar Membership	No
Additional Test Required	No
Certificate of Good Standing Required	Yes
Sponsor Required	Yes
Oath Required	Yes, in person. Nonresidents may be sworn in by judge in their district.
Fee	$175

Pro Hac Vice Admission

If not admitted to practice in the Northern District of Texas, you may represent a party in proceedings in this district only by permission of the presiding judge.
Submit court form, Certificate of Good Standing and $25 filing fee.

Address
Clerk of Court, U.S. District Court
Earle Cabell Federal Building and U.S. Courthouse
1100 Commerce Street, Room 1452
Dallas, TX 75242

Telephone
214-753-2190

District Court Website
www.txnd.uscourts.gov

Bankruptcy Court Admission

Regular: The Court follows the District Court rules of admission.
Pro Hac Vice: Motions to appear *pro hac vice* shall be filed with the clerk and presented to the presiding bankruptcy judge. $25 application fee.

Bankruptcy Court Website
www.txnb.uscourts.gov

Telephone
214-753-2000

U.S. District Court – Texas Southern District

Authorized Active Judges	Circuit
19	5

Bob Casey United States Courthouse. Photo: U.S. DOJ

Admission

State Bar Membership Required	Any U.S. State, District of Columbia or Territory. If not member of Texas bar must also be a member of a U.S. District Court.
Automatic Admission with State Bar Membership	No
Additional Test Required	No, but an approved applicant must attend a workshop held by the court before being admitted unless they reside outside the District and have provided a Certificate of Good Standing
Certificate of Good Standing Required	Yes
Sponsor Required	Yes (2)
Oath Required	Yes
Fee	$150. Members must reapply every 5 years from the date of admission by filing a Renewal Questionnaire.

Pro Hac Vice Admission

A lawyer who is not admitted to practice before this court may appear as attorney-in-charge for a party in a case in this court with the permission of the judge before whom the case is pending. When a lawyer who is not a member of the bar of this court first appears in a case, the lawyer shall move for leave to appear as attorney-in-charge for the client using the Motion for Admission *Pro Hac Vice* form.

Address
Attorney Admissions
United States District Court
P.O. Box 61010
Houston, TX 77208-1010

Telephone
713-250-5500

District Court Website
www.txsd.uscourts.gov

Bankruptcy Court Admission

See District Court rules above. No fee.

Bankruptcy Court Website
www.txsb.uscourts.gov

Telephone
713-250-5500

U.S. District Court – Texas Western District

Authorized Active Judges	Circuit
13	5

John H. Wood, Jr. U.S. Courthouse. Photo: U.S. DOJ

Admission

State Bar Membership Required	Any state. An applicant who is not licensed to practice by any state may apply for admission, however, if admitted, such an attorney must obtain a license from the highest court of any state within one year after being admitted to the bar of this Court.
Auto Admission with State Bar	No
Additional Test Required	No. Within 1 year before application is filed, the applicant must complete a live, video or on-line CLE program on federal court practice approved by the court. Not applicable for non-residents admitted to another U.S. District Court.
Cert. of Good Standing Required	Yes
Sponsor Required	Yes. 2 letters of reference from members of District where applicant resides.
Oath Required	Yes, in person. Nonresidents may be sworn in by judge in their district.
Fee	$170. Renewal fee of $25 every 3 years.

Pro Hac Vice Admission

An attorney who is licensed by the highest court of a state or another federal district court, but who is not admitted to practice before this court, may represent a party in this court *pro hac vice* only by permission of the judge presiding. $25 fee.
Unless excused by the judge presiding, an attorney is ordinarily required to apply for admission to the bar of this court.

Address
Clerk, U.S. District Court
655 East Durango Boulevard, Room G-65
San Antonio, TX 78206

Telephone
210-472-6550
District Court Website
www.txwd.uscourts.gov

Bankruptcy Court Admission

Regular: An attorney seeking to practice before the Bankruptcy Court for the Western District of Texas must make application to the U.S. District Court for the Western District of Texas.
Pro Hac Vice: Admission to practice *pro hac vice* before the district's bankruptcy court rests in the sole discretion of the bankruptcy judge to whom the motion is addressed. No fee.

Bankruptcy Court Website
www.txwb.uscourts.gov

Telephone
210-472-6720

U.S. Court of Appeals for the Sixth Circuit

Authorized Active Judges	Circuit
16	6

Potter Stewart U.S. Courthouse. Photo: U.S. Ct. Appeals for Sixth Circuit

Admission

Bar/Court Membership Required	Any state, another U.S. Court of Appeals, Supreme Court of the United States, or a U.S. District Court
Additional Test Required	No
Certificate of Good Standing Required	No, unless no Sponsor moving application
Sponsor Required	Yes, unless submitting Certificate of Good Standing
Oath Required	Yes
Fee	$200

Address
Office of the Clerk
U.S. Court of Appeals for the Sixth Circuit
540 Potter Stewart U.S. Courthouse
100 East Fifth Street
Cincinnati, OH 45202

Telephone
513-564-7000

Appeals Court Website
www.ca6.uscourts.gov

U.S. District Court – Kentucky Eastern District

Authorized Active Judges	Circuit
6	6

Scott Reed Federal Building & Courthouse. Photo: U.S. Ct. Appeals for Sixth Circuit

Admission

State Bar Membership Required	Kentucky
Automatic Admission with State Bar Membership	No
Additional Test Required	No
Certificate of Good Standing Required	No. Authorization and Release Form for investigation required.
Sponsor Required	Yes
Oath Required	Yes
Fee	$180

Pro Hac Vice Admission

An attorney who has not been admitted to the Bar of the Court, but who is in good standing in the Bar of any state, territory, or the District of Columbia, may request permission to practice in a particular case by filing the following with the Clerk:

(1) a motion for admission *pro hac vice*;

(2) an affidavit identifying the Bar in which the attorney is a member;

(3) the prescribed fee of $65;

(4) a written consent to be subject to the jurisdiction and rules of the Kentucky Supreme Court governing professional conduct; and

(5) a statement identifying the method of training completed before use of the Court's electronic filing system.

Address
Clerk, U.S. District Court
101 Barr Street, Suite 206
P.O. Drawer 3074
Lexington, KY 40588-3074

Telephone
859-233-2503

District Court Website
www.kyed.uscourts.gov

Bankruptcy Court Admission

See District Court rules above. $65 fee.

Bankruptcy Court Website
www.kyeb.uscourts.gov

Telephone
859-233-2608

U.S. District Court – Kentucky Western District

Authorized Active Judges	Circuit
5	6

Gene Snyder U.S. Courthouse. Photo: U.S. GSA by Bob Hower

Admission

State Bar Membership Required	Kentucky
Automatic Admission with State Bar Membership	No
Additional Test Required	No
Certificate of Good Standing Required	No. Authorization and Release Form for investigation required.
Sponsor Required	Yes
Oath Required	Yes
Fee	$180

Pro Hac Vice Admission

An attorney who has not been admitted to the Bar of the Court, but who is in good standing in the Bar of any state, territory, or the District of Columbia, may request permission to practice in a particular case by filing the following with the Clerk:
(1) a motion for admission *pro hac vice*;
(2) an affidavit identifying the Bar in which the attorney is a member;
(3) the prescribed fee of $65;
(4) a written consent to be subject to the jurisdiction and rules of the Kentucky Supreme Court governing professional conduct; and
(5) a statement identifying the method of training completed before use of the Court's electronic filing system.

Address
Clerk, U.S. District Court
Gene Snyder U.S. Courthouse
601 West Broadway, Suite 106
Louisville, KY 40202-2238

Telephone
502-625-3500

District Court Website
www.kywd.uscourts.gov

Bankruptcy Court Admission

See District Court rules above. No fee.

Bankruptcy Court Website
www.kywb.uscourts.gov

Telephone
502-627-5800

U.S. District Court – Michigan Eastern District

Authorized Active Judges	Circuit
15	6

Theodore Levin U.S. Courthouse. Photo: U.S. Dist. Ct. Eastern Michigan

Admission

State Bar Membership Required	Any state, territory, District of Columbia or U.S. District Court
Automatic Admission with State Bar Membership	No
Additional Test Required	No
Certificate of Good Standing Required	Yes
Sponsor Required	No
Oath Required	Yes, in person
Fee	$200

Pro Hac Vice Admission

The Eastern District of Michigan **does not grant *pro hac vice* admission**. Exceptions have been made for multi-district litigation, appointed counsel in death penalty cases and for good cause, at the discretion of the Judge.
Even if you have retained local counsel, if you plan to submit documents under your signature, submitting signed documents is considered "practice in this court" and requires admission.

Address
Clerk's Office
U.S. District Court
231 W. Lafayette Blvd.
Detroit, MI 48226

Telephone
313-234-5044

District Court Website
www.mied.uscourts.gov

Bankruptcy Court Admission

Except as otherwise provided by law, appearance before the court on behalf of a person or entity may be made only by an attorney admitted to the bar of, or permitted to practice before, the U.S. District Court for the Eastern District of Michigan.
See Local Rules for list of actions that do not constitute the practice of law.

Bankruptcy Court Website
www.mieb.uscourts.gov

Telephone
313-234-0068

U.S. District Court – Michigan Western District

Authorized Active Judges	Circuit
4	6

Gerald R. Ford Federal Building. Photo: U.S. Dist. Ct. Western Michigan

Admission

State Bar Membership Required	Any state
Automatic Admission with State Bar Membership	No
Additional Test Required	No
Certificate of Good Standing Required	Yes
Sponsor Required	Yes, but newly admitted attorney of a state may request a waiver. For applicants residing in another state, the sponsor may be a judge of a court of record of that state, or a federal judge.
Oath Required	Yes
Fee	$200

Pro Hac Vice Admission

This Court **disfavors** *pro hac vice* admission and prefers lawyers appearing before it become full members of the bar of the Court. *Pro hac vice* admission may be allowed on a temporary basis pending full admission, or in unusual circumstances.

Address
Clerk, U.S. District Court
399 Federal Building
110 Michigan St., N.W.
Grand Rapids, MI 49503

Telephone
616-456-2381

District Court Website
www.miwd.uscourts.gov

Bankruptcy Court Admission

An attorney or law student who is admitted to practice in the U.S. District Court for the Western District of Michigan is admitted to practice in the Court.

(1) All attorneys licensed to practice law in Michigan must apply for admission to practice before the U.S. District Court for the Western District of Michigan and may not apply for *pro hac vice* admission. (2) All attorneys licensed to practice in a state other than Michigan and who maintain a regular office within the State of Michigan must apply for admission to practice before the U.S. District Court for the Western District of Michigan and may not apply for *pro hac vice* admission. (3) Licensed attorneys not subject to subparagraphs (1) and (2) above may apply for *pro hac vice* admission by filing motion with $35 fee.

Bankruptcy Court Website
www.miwb.uscourts.gov

Telephone
616-456-2693

U.S. District Court – Ohio Northern District

Authorized Active Judges	Circuit
12	6

Carl B. Stokes U.S. Court House. Photo: U.S. Dist. Ct. Ohio Northern Dist.

Admission

State Bar Membership Required	Any state, DC, or U.S. District Court
Automatic Admission with State Bar Membership	No
Additional Test Required	No, but unless admitted to Southern District of Ohio for past 2 years, must take a seminar on federal district court practice
Certificate of Good Standing Required	Yes
Sponsor Required	Yes (2), unless admitted to the Southern District of Ohio for past 2 years
Oath Required	Yes
Fee	$190

Pro Hac Vice Admission

The Court's **strong preference is that attorneys seek permanent admission** to the Bar of this Court, however, any member of the Bar of any court of the United States or of any state may, upon written or oral motion and payment of the $100 *pro hac vice* admission fee, be permitted to appear and participate in a particular case.
A certificate of good standing not older than 30 days from the aforementioned court(s) or an affidavit swearing to applicant's current good standing must accompany the motion.

Address
U.S. District Court, Northern District of Ohio
Carl B. Stokes U.S. Courthouse
801 West Superior Avenue
Cleveland, OH 44113-1830

Telephone
216-357-7000

District Court Website
www.ohnd.uscourts.gov

Bankruptcy Court Admission

Regular: Every member in good standing of the Bar of the U.S. District Court for the Northern District of Ohio is entitled to practice before this Court.
Pro Hac Vice: Any member of the Bar of any court of the United States or of any state may, upon written or oral motion, be permitted to participate in a case or proceeding. Unless otherwise ordered by the Court, it shall not be necessary for any attorney entitled to practice before the Court or permitted to appear and participate in a case or proceeding to associate with or to designate an attorney with an office in this district upon whom notices, rulings, and communications may be served. No fee.

Bankruptcy Court Website
www.ohnb.uscourts.gov

Telephone
216-615-4300

U.S. District Court – Ohio Southern District

Authorized Active Judges	Circuit
8	6

Joseph P. Kinneary U.S. Courthouse Photos: U.S. GSA by Carol M. Highsmith, Inc.

Admission

State Bar Membership Required	Ohio, unless member of U.S. District Court of Ohio Northern District for past 2 years
Automatic Admission with State Bar	No
Additional Test Required	Yes. Exam administered by Federal Bar Assn. on Federal Rules of Civil Procedure, Evidence, Jurisdiction, Venue and Local Rules of Court.
Certificate of Good Standing Required	No, unless member of U.S. District Court of Ohio Northern District for past 2 years
Sponsor Required	Yes (2), unless member of U.S. District Court of Ohio Northern District for past 2 years
Oath Required	Yes
Fee	$150

Pro Hac Vice Admission

Member of any State, not otherwise eligible for admission to the Bar of this Court, may, upon written motion, approval of the Court, and payment of the *pro hac vice* admission fee, be permitted to appear and participate in a particular case, or in a group of related cases.
A motion for permission to appear *pro hac vice* shall be accompanied by a current certificate of good standing from any state, and the $200 fee.

Address
260 Joseph P. Kinneary Courthouse
85 Marconi Boulevard
Columbus, OH 43215

Telephone
614-719-3000
District Court Website
www.ohsd.uscourts.gov

Bankruptcy Court Admission

Regular: Admission to practice in the U.S. District Court for the Southern District of Ohio.
Pro Hac Vice: Membership in any state and admission to practice in any U.S. District Court shall be a prerequisite to practice in the bankruptcy court. Motion must be filed. No fee.

Bankruptcy Court Website
www.ohsb.uscourts.gov

Telephone
513-684-2572

U.S. District Court – Tennessee Eastern District

Authorized Active Judges	Circuit
5	6

Howard H. Baker Jr. U.S. Courthouse. Photo: U.S. Ct. Appeals for Sixth Circuit

Admission

State Bar Membership Required	Any state or District of Columbia
Automatic Admission with State Bar Membership	No
Additional Test Required	No
Certificate of Good Standing Required	Yes, if not admitted in Tennessee
Sponsor Required	Yes (2)
Oath Required	Yes, in person
Fee	$160

Pro Hac Vice Admission

Upon motion, attorneys who are members of the bar of the highest court of a state, territory or the District of Columbia and who are admitted to and entitled to practice in another U.S. District Court may be permitted to practice specially in this district *pro hac vice* in a particular case, provided (1) it is certified by the clerk or other duly authorized official that the attorney is a member of the state, territory or the District of Columbia bar, and (2) it is certified by the presiding judge or clerk of the other district court that the attorney is a member of that court's bar. $60 filing fee.

Attorneys not admitted to the bar of another U.S. District Court and who have an application pending may be admitted *pro hac vice* upon motion without payment of a fee, provided they file an affidavit of their application for admission to the bar of this Court and a Certificate of Good Standing not more than 30 days old from the highest court of a state, territory, or the District of Columbia.

Address
Clerk, U.S. District Court
Howard H. Baker Jr. U.S. Courthouse
800 Market Street, Suite 130
Knoxville, TN 37902

Telephone
865-545-4228

District Court Website
www.tned.uscourts.gov

Bankruptcy Court Admission

Regular: The bar of this court consists of all attorneys admitted to practice and in good standing with the U.S. District Court for the Eastern District of Tennessee.

Pro Hac Vice: An attorney who is in good standing as a member of the bar of a state and is admitted to practice in a U.S. District Court may be admitted *pro hac vice* by comity to appear before this court in a particular case, contested matter, or adversary proceeding. Admission *pro hac vice* must be sought by written motion. No fee.

Bankruptcy Court Website
www.tneb.uscourts.gov

Telephone
865-545-4279

U.S. District Court – Tennessee Middle District

Authorized Active Judges	Circuit
4	6

Estes Kefauver Federal Building & U.S. Courthouse. Photo: U.S. Ct. Appeals for Sixth Circuit

Admission

State Bar Membership Required	Tennessee
Automatic Admission with State Bar Membership	No
Additional Test Required	No
Certificate of Good Standing Required	No, unless *pro hac vice*
Sponsor Required	Yes (2), 1 in person
Oath Required	Yes
Fee	$200

Pro Hac Vice Admission

Any member in good standing of the bar of any other U.S. District Court who is not a resident of this district and who does not maintain an office in this district for the practice of law, may be permitted to appear and participate in a particular case in this Court subject to providing a Certificate of Good Standing or meeting other exceptions. $75 fee.

Address
U.S. District Court, Middle District of Tennessee
Office of the Clerk
801 Broadway, Room 800
Nashville, TN 37203

Telephone
615-736-5498

District Court Website
www.tnmd.uscourts.gov

Bankruptcy Court Admission

Regular: Unless under an exception to the rules, appearance before the Court may be made only by an attorney admitted to practice before the U.S. District Court for the Middle District of Tennessee.

Pro Hac Vice: Any attorney not admitted to practice before the U.S. District Court for the Middle District of Tennessee shall file a motion and proposed order with the U.S. Bankruptcy Court for the Middle District of Tennessee for permission to appear *pro hac vice*. Any attorney admitted to appear *pro hac vice* who does not have a principal law office in the State of Tennessee shall obtain local counsel who is admitted to practice in the U.S. District Court for the Middle District of Tennessee and who has a principal law office in Tennessee. No fee.

Bankruptcy Court Website
www.tnmb.uscourts.gov

Telephone
615-736-5584

U.S. District Court – Tennessee Western District

Authorized Active Judges	Circuit
5	6

Clifford Davis and Odell Horton Federal Building. Photo: U.S. Ct. Appeals for Sixth Circuit

Admission

State Bar Membership Required	Any state or District of Columbia
Automatic Admission with State Bar Membership	No
Additional Test Required	No
Certificate of Good Standing Required	No, unless *pro hac vice*
Sponsor Required	Yes
Oath Required	Yes
Fee	$150

Pro Hac Vice Admission

An attorney not licensed to practice law in the State of Tennessee, but who is licensed to practice and is in good standing in the bar of the highest court of any other state or of any federal district court, may be admitted specially for the purpose of acting as attorney in a case in this court. Any attorney seeking special admission shall submit motion, Certificate of Good Standing and $100 fee.

Address
Office of the Clerk
U.S. District Court
167 North Main Street, Room 242
Memphis, TN 38103

Telephone
901-495-1200

District Court Website
www.tnwd.uscourts.gov

Bankruptcy Court Admission

Regular: The Bar of this Court shall consist of all present members and those attorneys hereafter admitted to practice before the United States District Court for the Western District of Tennessee.

Pro Hac Vice: Any attorney who is in good standing as a member of the Bar of another state may be admitted *pro hac vice* by comity, upon a proper showing of qualifications, to handle a particular case or proceeding before this Court. Admission *pro hac vice* is by written motion accompanied by movant's declaration, signed under penalty of perjury, asserting good standing in the state and federal bars where movant maintains a law office. A proposed order and the $10 fee shall accompany the motion.

Bankruptcy Court Website
www.tnwb.uscourts.gov

Telephone
901-328-3500

Bankruptcy Appellate Panel for the Sixth Circuit

Admission

Any attorney admitted to practice before a United States District Court within the Sixth Circuit or before the United States Court of Appeals for the Sixth Circuit and who is in good standing before such court shall be deemed admitted to practice before the Bankruptcy Appellate Panel.

Pro Hac Vice Admission

An attorney not admitted as described above may apply to the panel for permission to appear in a particular appeal.

Address
U.S. Bankruptcy Appellate Panel for the Sixth Circuit
540 Potter Stewart U.S. Courthouse
100 East Fifth Street
Cincinnati, OH 45202-3988

Telephone
513-564-7000

BAP Website
www.ca6.uscourts.gov/internet/bap/bap.htm

U.S. Court of Appeals for the Seventh Circuit

Authorized Active Judges	Circuit
11	7

Everett M. Dirksen U.S. Courthouse. Photos: U.S. GSA; U.S. GSA by Hedrick Blessing

Admission

Bar/Court Membership Required	Any state, another U.S. Court of Appeals, Supreme Court of the United States, or a U.S. District Court
Additional Test Required	No
Certificate of Good Standing Required	No
Sponsor Required	Yes
Oath Required	Yes
Fee	$165

Address
Clerk
U.S. Court of Appeals for the Seventh Circuit
219 S. Dearborn Street
Room 2722
Chicago, IL 60604

Seventh Circuit Bar Association
www.7thcircuitbar.org

Telephone
312-435-5850

Appeals Court Website
www.ca7.uscourts.gov

U.S. District Court – Illinois Central District

Authorized Active Judges	Circuit
4	7

Admission

State Bar Membership Required	Any state or District of Columbia
Automatic Admission with State Bar Membership	No
Additional Test Required	No
Certificate of Good Standing Required	No, unless making your own motion based on admission to another state or another Illinois U.S. District Court
Sponsor Required	Only required if applicant is not making his/her own motion based on membership in another state or Illinois U.S. District Court
Oath Required	Yes
Fee	$185

Pro Hac Vice Admission

The court **does not permit *pro hac vice* admissions generally**.
At the discretion of the presiding judge, an attorney who is duly licensed to practice in any state or the District of Columbia may file a motion seeking leave to participate in a case while his or her application for admission to practice in the Central District of Illinois is pending. The application for admission must be submitted contemporaneously with the motion for leave.

Address
Office of the Clerk
U.S. District Court, Central District of Illinois
600 East Monroe
151 Federal Building
Springfield, IL 62701

Telephone
217-492-4020

District Court Website
www.ilcd.uscourts.gov

Bankruptcy Court Admission

Regular: Attorneys who intend to practice before this Court must be licensed to practice in the Central District of Illinois.
Pro Hac Vice: Admission *Pro hac vice* may, upon motion, be granted for appearance in a case on **one occasion.**

Bankruptcy Court Website
www.ilcb.uscourts.gov

Telephone
217-492-4551

U.S. District Court – Illinois Northern District

Authorized Active Judges	Circuit
22	7

Admission

State Bar Membership Required	Any state or District of Columbia
Automatic Admission with State Bar Membership	No
Additional Test Required	No, but the Court has a "General Bar" and a "Trial Bar". Applicants to Trial Bar must provide evidence of having the requisite trial experience. See Local Rules for distinctions.
Certificate of Good Standing Required	Yes
Sponsor Required	Yes (2) from any state or District of Columbia. Or, members of another U.S. District Court in Illinois may make their own motion (for admission to General Bar).
Oath Required	Yes
Fee	General Bar: $150 Trial Bar: $50. Trial Bar members must also be General Bar members.

Pro Hac Vice Admission

A member of the bar of the highest court of any state or of any U.S. District Court may, upon motion, be permitted to argue or try a particular case in whole or in part.
An attorney not having an office within this District ("nonresident attorney") shall appear before this Court only upon having designated as local counsel a member of the bar of this Court having an office within this District upon whom service of papers may be made. Such designation shall be made at the time the initial notice or pleading is filed by the nonresident attorney. Local counsel shall file an appearance but is not required to participate in the case beyond the extent required of an attorney designated pursuant to this rule.

Address
U.S. District Court, Northern District of Illinois
219 S. Dearborn St., Room 2050
Chicago, IL 60604

Telephone
312-435-5670
District Court Website
www.ilnd.uscourts.gov

Bankruptcy Court Admission

Regular: An attorney appearing before this court must be admitted to practice before the District Court. See Local Bankruptcy Rule 2090-1 for "Circumstances Under Which Trial Bar Membership Required".
Pro Hac Vice: An attorney who is not a member of the bar of the District Court but who is a member of the bar of the highest court of any state or of any U.S. District Court may appear before this court after: (1) completing application for leave to appear *pro hac vice* as prescribed by the District Court, (2) paying the required $50 fee to the Clerk of the District Court, and (3) filing the application and receipt for payment with the Clerk of this court. No order of court is required.

Bankruptcy Court Website
www.ilnb.uscourts.gov

Telephone
312-435-5694

U.S. District Court – Illinois Southern District

Authorized Active Judges	Circuit
4	7

Admission

State Bar Membership Required	Any state of the District of Columbia
Automatic Admission with State Bar Membership	No
Additional Test Required	No
Certificate of Good Standing Required	Yes, unless using a local sponsor to move application
Sponsor Required	Only required if applicant is not making his/her own motion based on membership in another state or another Illinois U.S. District Court
Oath Required	Yes
Fee	$200

Pro Hac Vice Admission

Any attorney licensed to practice law in any state of the United States or the District of Columbia who does not wish to be admitted generally but wishes to be admitted for the purposes of a specific civil or criminal case only may, upon submission of a Motion to Appear *Pro Hac Vice* which contains a verified statement setting forth the state and federal bars of which the movant is a member in good standing, the bar number, if any, issued by each jurisdiction, and the required filing fee of $100 for *pro hac vice* motions, be permitted to appear of record and participate *pro hac vice*.
It shall not be necessary for parties appearing by non-resident counsel to retain local counsel to represent them. At any time for good cause, upon the motion of any party, or upon its own motion, the Court may require that a non-resident attorney obtain local counsel to assist in the case.
Recently paid $100 *pro hac vice* fee may be applied towards full admission fee.

Address
Clerk, U.S. District Court
Melvin Price Federal Building and U.S. Courthouse
750 Missouri Avenue, Room 104
East St. Louis, IL 62201

Telephone
618-482-9371

District Court Website
www.ilsd.uscourts.gov

Bankruptcy Court Admission

Regular: Admission of attorneys to practice generally in the Southern District of Illinois is accomplished through the U.S. District Court.
Pro Hac Vice: A Motion to Appear *Pro Hac Vice* is filed with the U.S. Bankruptcy Court with the $100 fee tendered to the Clerk of the U.S. District Court. A proposed order is not required for this type of motion.

Bankruptcy Court Website
www.ilsb.uscourts.gov

Telephone
618-482-9400

U.S. District Court – Indiana Northern District

Authorized Active Judges	Circuit
5	7

Robert A. Grant Federal Building & U.S. Courthouse. Photo: U.S. GSA

Admission

State Bar Membership Required	Any state or U.S. Supreme Court
Automatic Admission with State Bar Membership	No
Additional Test Required	No
Certificate of Good Standing Required	Yes, from **each** state
Sponsor Required	Yes
Oath Required	Yes
Fee	$160

Pro Hac Vice Admission

Requirements: Attorney admitted to practice in any other United States Court or the highest court of any state, is a member in good standing of the bar of every jurisdiction to which the applicant is admitted to practice, is not currently under suspension, has certified that he or she will abide by the local rules of this court and the Seventh Circuit Standards of Professional Conduct, has made application to this court, has made payment of the $80 fee, and has been granted leave by this court to appear in a specific action.
Whenever necessary to facilitate the conduct of litigation, this court may require any attorney appearing in any action who resides outside this district to retain as local counsel a member of the bar of this court who is resident of this district.

Address
Clerk, U.S. District Court
102 Robert A. Grant Courthouse
204 South Main Street
South Bend, IN 46601

Telephone
574-246-8000

District Court Website
www.innd.uscourts.gov

Bankruptcy Court Admission

Regular: The bar of this court shall consist of those persons admitted to practice by the U.S. District Court for the Northern District of Indiana.
Pro Hac Vice: Must be an attorney admitted to practice in any other U.S. Court or the highest court of any state and who is, on application to this court, granted leave to appear in a specific action *pro hac vice* and who tenders the required $80 fee.

Bankruptcy Court Website
www.innb.uscourts.gov

Telephone
574-968-2100

U.S. District Court – Indiana Southern District

Authorized Active Judges	Circuit
5	7

Birch Bayh Federal Building & U.S. Courthouse. Photos: U.S. GSA by Carol M. Highsmith, Inc.

Admission

State Bar Membership Required	Any state or U.S. Supreme Court
Automatic Admission with State Bar Membership	No
Additional Test Required	No
Certificate of Good Standing Required	Yes, for sponsor to verify
Sponsor Required	Yes
Oath Required	Yes
Fee	$160

Pro Hac Vice Admission

Admission *pro hac vice* may be sought upon written motion accompanied by the $30 fee, and supported by the movant's affidavit that he or she is admitted to practice before the highest court of the jurisdiction in which he or she customarily practices and is not currently under suspension or other disciplinary action with respect to his or her practice.

Address
Clerk, U.S. District Court, Indiana Southern District
Birch Bayh Federal Building & U.S. Courthouse
46 East Ohio Street, Room 105
Indianapolis, IN 46204

Telephone
317-229-3700

District Court Website
www.insd.uscourts.gov

Bankruptcy Court Admission

Regular: The bar of this Court shall consist of those persons admitted to practice in the Southern District of Indiana.

Pro Hac Vice: In order to obtain leave of this Court to appear in a specific action, an attorney must file with the Court a Motion to Appear *Pro Hac Vice*. If not admitted to practice in the State of Indiana, include an affidavit that substantially complies with the form available on the Court's website and $30 *pro hac vice* fee.

Bankruptcy Court Website
www.insb.uscourts.gov

Telephone
317-229-3800

U.S. District Court – Wisconsin Eastern District

Authorized Active Judges	Circuit
5	7

Federal Building & U.S. Courthouse. Photos: U.S. GSA by: Edward Purcell; Skot Weidemann

Admission

State Bar Membership Required	Any state, District of Columbia or U.S. Court
Automatic Admission with State Bar Membership	No
Additional Test Required	No
Certificate of Good Standing Required	Yes, unless no sponsor
Sponsor Required	No, unless not submitting Certificate of Good Standing
Oath Required	Yes
Fee	$185

Pro Hac Vice Admission

Pro hac vice motions for admission **are not permitted**.

Address
U.S. District Court, Wisconsin Eastern District
362 U.S. Courthouse
517 E. Wisconsin Avenue
Milwaukee, WI 53202

Telephone
414-297-1205

District Court Website
www.wied.uscourts.gov

Bankruptcy Court Admission

Regular: The U.S. Bankruptcy Court for the Eastern District of Wisconsin limits practice before it to attorneys admitted to the District Court for the Eastern District of Wisconsin.

Pro Hac Vice: Attorneys appearing in bankruptcy court shall comply with rules for admission to practice before the U.S. District Court for the Eastern District of Wisconsin, except that the bankruptcy court in its discretion, upon request from counsel and without application, fee, or motion of a member in good standing, may issue an order allowing appearance by an attorney who is not admitted to practice in this district for matters that are incidental and limited in duration. Contact the Clerk for admission procedures. No fee.

Bankruptcy Court Website
www.wieb.uscourts.gov

Telephone
414-297-3291

U.S. District Court – Wisconsin Western District

Authorized Active Judges	Circuit
2	7

Robert W. Kastenmeier U.S. Courthouse. Photo: U.S. GSA

Admission

State Bar Membership Required	Any state, District of Columbia or U.S. Court
Automatic Admission with State Bar Membership	No
Additional Test Required	No
Certificate of Good Standing Required	No
Sponsor Required	Yes
Oath Required	Yes
Fee	$150

Pro Hac Vice Admission

By permission of a judge or magistrate judge, any lawyer eligible for membership in the bar of this court may proceed in a particular matter without becoming a member of the bar of this court.
Non-resident lawyers need not retain local counsel to assist in the presentation of their cases unless specifically directed to do so by a judge or magistrate judge.

Address
Clerk, United States District Court
P.O. Box 432
Madison, WI 53701

Telephone
608-264-5156
District Court Website
www.wiwd.uscourts.gov

Western District of Wisconsin Bar Association
www.wdbar.org

Bankruptcy Court Admission

Regular: Members of the Court are those admitted to the U.S. District Court for the Western District of Wisconsin.
Pro Hac Vice: See District Court rules above. No fee.

Bankruptcy Court Website
www.wiwb.uscourts.gov

Telephone
608-264-5178

U.S. Court of Appeals for the Eighth Circuit

Authorized Active Judges	Circuit
11	8

Thomas F. Eagleton U.S. Courthouse. Photo: U.S. GSA

Admission

Bar/Court Membership Required	Any state, another U.S. Court of Appeals, Supreme Court of the United States, or a U.S. District Court
Additional Test Required	No
Certificate of Good Standing Required	No
Sponsor Required	Yes
Oath Required	Yes
Fee	$190

Address
U.S. Court of Appeals for the Eighth Circuit
Thomas F. Eagleton United States Courthouse
111 South Tenth Street, Room 24.329
St. Louis, MO 63102-1116

Telephone
314-244-2400

Appeals Court Website
www.ca8.uscourts.gov

Assn. of the Bar of the United States Court of Appeals for the Eighth Circuit
www.eighthcircuitbar.com

U.S. District Court – Arkansas Eastern District

Authorized Active Judges	Circuit
5	8

Admission

State Bar Membership Required	(1) Licensed to practice in state of residence, if not Arkansas must be a member of any U.S. District Court; (2) **members of U.S. District Court for Western Arkansas are automatically enrolled in this District**.
Automatic Admission with State Bar Membership	No
Additional Test Required	No
Certificate of Good Standing Required	Yes, from state where attorney resides and a U.S. District Court
Sponsor Required	In-State Attorneys: Yes Out-of-State Attorneys: No
Oath Required	Yes
Fee	$160

Pro Hac Vice Admission

Any attorney who is a member in good standing of the Bar of any U.S. District Court, or of the highest court of any state or territory or insular possession of the United States, but is not admitted to practice in the District Courts in Arkansas, may, upon oral or written application, be permitted to appear and participate in a particular case.
The application shall designate a member who maintains an office in Arkansas for the practice of law with whom the court and opposing counsel may readily communicate regarding the case. There shall also be filed with such application the address and telephone number of the named designee. [May be waived at the discretion of the Court]

Address
Clerk of Court
U.S. District Court, Eastern District of Arkansas
600 West Capitol Avenue, Room A149
Little Rock, AR 72201

Telephone
501-604-5351

District Court Website
www.are.uscourts.gov

Bankruptcy Court Admission

Regular: The bar of this Court shall consist of all attorneys admitted to practice before the U.S. District Court for the **Eastern and Western Districts of Arkansas** unless said attorney has been specifically suspended or disbarred by the Court.
Pro Hac Vice: Any attorney who is a member of the bar of another state may be admitted *pro hac vice* in a particular case before this Court. The written motion must be accompanied by movant's declaration asserting good standing in the state bar where movant maintains a law office. The applicant shall designate a member of the bar of this Court who maintains an office in the Eastern or Western District of Arkansas as local counsel. The Court may waive the requirement for local counsel upon written motion. See exceptions for attorneys appearing in the United States District Court in the Texarkana Division of the Western District of Arkansas who reside in Texarkana, Texas. No fee.

Bankruptcy Court Website
www.areb.uscourts.gov

Telephone
501-918-5500

U.S. District Court – Arkansas Western District

Authorized Active Judges	Circuit
3	8

Admission

State Bar Membership Required	(1) Licensed to practice in state of residence, if not Arkansas must be a member of any U.S. District Court; (2) **Members of U.S. Dist. Court for Eastern Arkansas are automatically enrolled in this District.**
Automatic Admission with State Bar Membership	No
Additional Test Required	No
Certificate of Good Standing Required	Yes, from state where attorney resides and a U.S. District Court
Sponsor Required	In-State Attorneys: Yes Out-of-State Attorneys: No
Oath Required	Yes
Fee	$160

Pro Hac Vice Admission

Any attorney who is a member in good standing of the Bar of any United States District Court, or of the highest court of any state or territory or insular possession of the United States, but is not admitted to practice in the District Courts in Arkansas, may, upon oral or written application, be permitted to appear and participate in a particular case.
The application shall designate a member of the Bar of these Courts who maintains an office in Arkansas for the practice of law with whom the court and opposing counsel may readily communicate regarding the case. [Court may waive local counsel requirement]

Address
Unites States District Court
P.O. Box 1547
Fort Smith, AR 72902-1547

Telephone
479-783-6833
District Court Website
www.arwd.uscourts.gov

Bankruptcy Court Admission

Regular: The bar of this Court shall consist of all attorneys admitted to practice before the U.S. District Court for the **Eastern and Western Districts of Arkansas** unless said attorney has been specifically suspended or disbarred by the Court.
Pro Hac Vice: Any attorney who is a member of the bar of another state may be admitted *pro hac vice* in a particular case before this Court. The written motion must be accompanied by movant's declaration asserting good standing in the state bar where movant maintains a law office. The applicant shall designate a member of the bar of this Court who maintains an office in the Eastern or Western District of Arkansas as local counsel. The Court may waive the requirement for local counsel upon written motion. See exceptions for attorneys appearing in the United States District Court in the Texarkana Division of the Western District of Arkansas who reside in Texarkana, Texas. No fee.

Bankruptcy Court Website
www.areb.uscourts.gov

Telephone
501-918-5500 (same as Eastern Dist.)

U.S. District Court – Iowa Northern District

Authorized Active Judges	Circuit
2	8

U.S. Courthouse. Photo: National Archives, RG 121-BS, Box 30, Folder N, Print 1

Admission

State Bar Membership Required	Iowa
Automatic Admission with State Bar Membership	No
Additional Test Required	No. Must have 6 hours of CLE in the federal practice area within last 2 years and biennially thereafter.
Certificate of Good Standing Required	No
Sponsor Required	Yes (2). One sponsor must be a sitting Iowa state judge or justice and the other a member of the Court.
Oath Required	Yes
Fee	$150

Pro Hac Vice Admission

A lawyer who is not a member of the bar of the district may be admitted to practice in a particular case *pro hac vice* by filing a motion. By asking to be admitted *pro hac vice*, the lawyer agrees that in connection with the lawyer's *pro hac vice* representation, the lawyer will submit to and comply with all provisions and requirements of the Iowa Rules of Professional Conduct, or any successor code adopted by the Iowa Supreme Court. $75 fee.

Address
Clerk of Court
U.S. District Court, District of Northern Iowa
4200 C Street, SW
Cedar Rapids, IA 52404

Telephone
319-286-2300

District Court Website
www.iand.uscourts.gov

Bankruptcy Court Admission

Regular: The bar of the Bankruptcy Court for the Northern District of Iowa shall consist of those attorneys who are admitted to practice and who remain in good standing before the U.S. District Court **for either the Northern or Southern District of Iowa**.

Pro Hac Vice: Upon written application to the bankruptcy court and in its discretion, an attorney who is not a member of the bar of the bankruptcy court may be permitted to appear and participate in a pending case and/or proceeding. Any attorney who is admitted *pro hac vice* must have associate counsel who is an active member of the bar of the bankruptcy court. On written motion and for good cause, the court may excuse compliance with the local-counsel requirement. No fee.

Bankruptcy Court Website
www.ianb.uscourts.gov

Telephone
319-286-2200

U.S. District Court – Iowa Southern District

Authorized Active Judges	Circuit
2	8

U.S. Courthouse. Photo: U.S. GSA

Admission

State Bar Membership Required	Iowa
Automatic Admission with State Bar Membership	No
Additional Test Required	No. Must have 6 hours of CLE in the federal practice area within last 2 years and biennially thereafter.
Certificate of Good Standing Required	No
Sponsor Required	Yes (2). One sponsor must be a sitting Iowa state judge or justice and the other a member of the Court.
Oath Required	Yes
Fee	$150

Pro Hac Vice Admission

A lawyer who is not a member of the bar of the district may be admitted to practice in a particular case *pro hac vice* by filing a motion. The lawyer agrees to comply with the Iowa Rules of Professional Conduct, or any successor code adopted by the Iowa Supreme Court

To be admitted *pro hac vice*, a lawyer must file a written motion and pay the $75 fee. See Local Rules for motion requirements.

Address
Clerk, U.S. District Court
P.O. Box 9344
Des Moines, IA 50309-9344

Telephone
515-284-6248
District Court Website
www.iasd.uscourts.gov

Bankruptcy Court Admission

See District Court rules. No fee for *pro hac vice* admission.

Bankruptcy Court Website
www.iasb.uscourts.gov

Telephone
515-284-6230

U.S. District Court – Minnesota District Court

Authorized Active Judges	Circuit
7	8

Warren E. Burger Federal Building & U.S. Courthouse. Photo: U.S. GSA

Admission

State Bar Membership Required	Minnesota
Automatic Admission with State Bar Membership	No
Additional Test Required	No
Certificate of Good Standing Required	No
Sponsor Required	Yes (2), 1 in person
Oath Required	Yes, in person
Fee	$175. Members must re-register and pay $40 fee every 3 years.

Pro Hac Vice Admission

Any attorney residing outside of this state and admitted to practice before another U.S. District Court, but not admitted to practice in the Supreme Court of this state, may, upon oral or written motion of a member of the bar of this Court, be permitted by this Court to appear as an attorney in the trial of any action or the hearing on any motion, petition or other proceeding then pending before this Court, but only if the attorney associates with an active member of the bar of this Court who shall participate in the preparation and trial of the case or presentation of the matter involved. The attorney with whom a non-member of the bar associates shall be a Minnesota resident unless the Court upon motion approves an association with a non-resident.

Motions for *pro hac vice* admission must be accompanied by a signed affidavit by the member of the bar of this Court and the attorney to be admitted *pro hac vice* on the Motion for Admission *Pro Hac Vice* form and payment of the $100 *pro hac vice* admission fee.

Address
U.S. District Court, District of Minnesota
Warren E. Burger Federal Building & U.S. Courthouse
316 North Robert Street, Suite 100
St. Paul, MN 55101

Telephone
651-848-1122

District Court Website
www.mnd.uscourts.gov

Bankruptcy Court Admission

Regular: The bar of this court consists of those attorneys admitted to practice before the U.S. District Court for this district.

Pro Hac Vice: Attorneys not admitted to practice in the district court may appear or file documents, other than proofs of claim, only after being admitted *pro hac vice*. $100 fee.

Bankruptcy Court Website
www.mnb.uscourts.gov

Telephone
612-664-5200

U.S. District Court – Missouri Eastern District

Authorized Active Judges	Circuit
9	8

Admission

State Bar Membership Required	Any state or District of Columbia
Automatic Admission with State Bar Membership	No
Additional Test Required	No
Certificate of Good Standing Required	Yes, from **each** state bar and federal court where admitted, whether active **or** inactive
Sponsor Required	Yes (2)
Oath Required	Yes, in person
Fee	$200

Pro Hac Vice Admission

An attorney who is not regularly admitted to the bar of this Court, but who is a member of the bar of the highest court of any state or the District of Columbia, may be admitted *pro hac vice* for the limited purpose of appearing in a specific pending action. Unless allowed by a judge for good cause, an attorney may not be granted admission *pro hac vice* if the applicant resides in the Eastern District of Missouri, is regularly employed in the Eastern District of Missouri, or is regularly engaged in the practice of law in the Eastern District of Missouri.

The movant attorney shall include as an attachment to the motion for admission *pro hac vice* a certificate of good standing from the jurisdiction in which the attorney resides or is regularly employed as an attorney, or other proof of good standing satisfactory to the court.

Address
Clerk, U.S. District Court
Eastern District of Missouri
Thomas F. Eagleton U.S. Courthouse
111 South 10th Street, 3rd Floor
St. Louis, MO 63102

Telephone
314-244-7914

District Court Website
www.moed.uscourts.gov

Bankruptcy Court Admission

Regular: The bar of this Court shall consist of any attorney in good standing to practice before the U.S. District Court for the Eastern District of Missouri.

Pro Hac Vice: An attorney who is not a member of this Court but is a member in good standing of the bar of the highest court of any state or the District of Columbia may be permitted to appear and file documents in a case before this Court only when admitted *pro hac vice* pursuant to applicable rules of the U.S. District Court for the Eastern District of Missouri. A motion together with the $100 fee must be submitted. The Court will consider such motions without hearing. The Court encourages visiting attorneys admitted *pro hac vice* to affiliate with local counsel.

Bankruptcy Court Website
www.moeb.uscourts.gov

Telephone
314-244-4500

U.S. District Court – Missouri Western District

Authorized Active Judges	Circuit
7	8

Charles Evan Whittaker Federal Courthouse. Photos: U.S. DOJ; U.S. DOE

Admission

State Bar Membership Required	Member of: (1) Missouri Bar, or (2) U.S. Dist. Court, District of Kansas
Automatic Admission with State Bar Membership	No
Additional Test Required	No
Certificate of Good Standing Required	No
Sponsor Required	(1) Yes, two with one in person to move application (2) No
Oath Required	(1) Yes, in person; (2) No
Fee	(1) $157; (2) $150. $10 annual renewal fee.

Pro Hac Vice Admission

Any attorney residing outside of this district and admitted in the U.S. District Court in the district of residence, may, upon written motion, be permitted by this Court to participate as an attorney in any proceeding then pending before this Court, but only if the attorney associates with an active Missouri resident member of this Bar who shall participate in the preparation and trial of the case and on whom service of all papers may be made. $50 fee.

Address
U.S. District Court, District of Western Missouri
131 West High Street
Jefferson City, MO 65101

Telephone
573-636-4015

District Court Website
www.mow.uscourts.gov

Bankruptcy Court Admission

Regular: Standards and requirements stated in the Local Rules of the District Court are adopted for attorney admission, discipline and unauthorized practice in the Bankruptcy Court.

If a party's counsel is a member of this Bar whose office is a great distance from court, counsel may be required to retain a local attorney who is a member of this Bar to be available for unscheduled meetings and hearings.

Pro Hac Vice: An attorney who is not a member of this Bar, but is a member of the Bar of any court of record, may be permitted to appear in a particular case. Visiting counsel shall file a Motion for Admission *Pro Hac Vice* designating a member of this Court with a law office in the District and division, upon whom service of all papers may be made. $50 fee.

Bankruptcy Court Website
www.mow.uscourts.gov/bankruptcy/

Telephone
816-512-5000

U.S. District Court – Nebraska

Authorized Active Judges	Circuit
3	8

Roman L. Hruska U.S. Courthouse. Image: U.S. GSA

Admission

State Bar Membership Required	Any state
Automatic Admission with State Bar Membership	No
Additional Test Required	No
Certificate of Good Standing Required	Yes
Sponsor Required	No
Oath Required	Yes
Fee	$150. $10 renewal every 2 years.

Pro Hac Vice Admission

An attorney admitted and licensed to practice before the highest court of any state may apply orally or in writing to a judge or the clerk to practice in this court for a particular case.
The attorney must (1) submit a certificate from the clerk of the highest court of any state in which the attorney is admitted to practice, and (2) take the prescribed oath.

Address
U.S. District Court
111 South 18th Plaza, Suite 1152
Omaha, NE 68102

Telephone
402-661-7350
District Court Website
www.ned.uscourts.gov

Bankruptcy Court Admission

The Court follows the District Court rules for admission. No fee.

Bankruptcy Court Website
www.neb.uscourts.gov

Telephone
402-661-7444

84

U.S. District Court – North Dakota

Authorized Active Judges	Circuit
2	8

William L. Guy Federal Building. Photo: U.S. DOJ

Admission

State Bar Membership Required	Any state or federal
Automatic Admission with State Bar Membership	No
Additional Test Required	No
Certificate of Good Standing Required	No
Sponsor Required	No
Oath Required	Yes
Fee	$200

Pro Hac Vice Admission

An attorney who is not admitted to practice before this court may be admitted to practice in a particular case by filing a motion seeking admission *pro hac vice*.
In addition, the attorney must pay an admission fee of $150.

Address
Office of the Clerk
United States District Court
P.O. Box 1193
Bismarck, ND 58502-1193

Telephone
701-530-2300

District Court Website
www.ndd.uscourts.gov

Bankruptcy Court Admission

The Court follows the District Court rules for admission. No fee.

Bankruptcy Court Website
www.ndb.uscourts.gov

Telephone
701-297-7100

U.S. District Court – South Dakota

Authorized Active Judges	Circuit
3	8

U.S. Courthouse. Photo: U.S. GSA by Carol M. Highsmith, Inc.

Admission

State Bar Membership Required	South Dakota
Automatic Admission with State Bar	No
Additional Test Required	No
Certificate of Good Standing Required	No
Sponsor Required	Yes (2 member references), 1 in person
Oath Required	Yes, in person
Fee	$200

Pro Hac Vice Admission

An attorney who is not a member of the bar of this court, but who is a member of the bar of another U.S. District Court, may participate in the conduct of a particular case, but such motion may be allowed only if the applicant associates with a member of the bar of this court. The attorney admitted to practice in this court shall be present during all proceedings in connection with the case, unless otherwise ordered, and shall have full authority to act for and on behalf of the client in all matters.

$100 fee. Note different divisions and judges may use different forms.

Address
Clerk, U.S. District Court
United States Courthouse
400 South Phillips Avenue, Room 128
Sioux Falls, SD 57104-6851

Telephone
605-330-6600

District Court Website
www.sdd.uscourts.gov

Bankruptcy Court Admission

The admission and practice of attorneys before this Court shall be governed by the rules as adopted by the U.S. District Court of South Dakota. $100 fee for *pro hac vice* admission.

Bankruptcy Court Website
www.sdb.uscourts.gov

Telephone
605-357-2400

Bankruptcy Appellate Panel for the Eight Circuit

Circuit
8

Admission

Any attorney admitted to practice before the Court of Appeals for the Eighth Circuit, and in good standing before that court, may practice before the United States Bankruptcy Appellate Panel for the Eighth Circuit. No separate admission fee shall be required.

Pro Hac Vice Admission

Counsel may file pleadings without being a member of the bar, but membership in the bar will be required to present oral argument before the Court.

Address
U.S. Bankruptcy Appellate Panel for the Eighth Circuit
Thomas F. Eagleton Courthouse
Room 24.329
111 South 10th Street
St. Louis, MO 63102

Telephone
314-244-2430

BAP Website
http://www.ca8.uscourts.gov/newbap/bapFrame.html

U.S. Court of Appeals for the Ninth Circuit

Authorized Active Judges	Circuit
29	9

James R. Browning U.S. Court of Appeals.
Photo: U.S. GSA

William Kenzo Nakamura U.S. Courthouse.
Photo: U.S. GSA by Carol M. Highsmith, Inc.

Admission

Bar/Court Membership Required	Any state, another U.S. Court of Appeals, Supreme Court of United States, or a U.S. District Court
Additional Test Required	No
Certificate of Good Standing Required	Yes, if court is providing sponsor
Sponsor Required	Yes, unless you attended a mass swearing-in ceremony in California
Oath Required	Yes
Fee	$190

Address
Attorney Admissions
U.S. Court of Appeals for the Ninth Circuit
P.O. Box 193939
San Francisco, CA 94119-3939

Telephone
415-355-7800

Appeals Court Website
www.ca9.uscourts.gov

U.S. District Court – Alaska

Authorized Active Judges	Circuit
3	9

Anchorage Federal Building. Photo: U.S. Dist. Ct. Alaska

Admission

State Bar Membership Required	Alaska
Automatic Admission with State Bar Membership	No
Additional Test Required	No
Certificate of Good Standing Required	Yes
Sponsor Required	No
Oath Required	Yes
Fee	$250

Pro Hac Vice Admission

A member of the bar of another jurisdiction, who is not an active member of this court, may, upon motion, be permitted to appear and participate on behalf of a party, but non-local counsel will ordinarily be required to associate with an active member of this court.

The court may permit a member in good standing of the bar of another jurisdiction, on a sufficient showing, to appear and participate without association with an active member of the bar of this court. $150 fee.

Address
U.S. District Court, District of Alaska
222 West Seventh Avenue, MS 4
Anchorage, AK 99513-7564
(must also serve petition for admission on Alaska Bar Association)

Telephone
907-677-6100
District Court Website
www.akd.uscourts.gov

Bankruptcy Court Admission

Regular: Any attorney who is admitted to practice law in the U.S. District Court for the District of Alaska is admitted to practice in this court.

Pro Hac Vice: Any attorney, who is a member of the bar of any U.S. court or any state or territory of the U.S., may be permitted upon ex parte application to appear in a particular case. A certificate of good standing from the state court or bar governing admission in the territory where the applicant has been admitted must be filed with the application. The court may waive the requirement of application by an attorney not admitted in the U.S. District Court for the District of Alaska in the interest of expediency and reduction of costs where the participation is limited and the matter is likely to be resolved without extensive hearings. The court may require designation of local counsel when appropriate (see Local Rules). No fee.

Bankruptcy Court Website
www.akb.uscourts.gov

Telephone
907-271-2655

U.S. District Court – Arizona

Authorized Active Judges	Circuit
13	9

Sandra Day O'Connor U.S. Courthouse. Photo: U.S. DOJ

Admission

State Bar Membership Required	Arizona
Automatic Admission with State Bar Membership	No
Additional Test Required	No
Certificate of Good Standing Required	No
Sponsor Required	Yes, in person
Oath Required	Yes
Fee	$180

Pro Hac Vice Admission

Any member of any Federal Court who neither resides nor maintains an office for the practice of law in the District of Arizona, may be admitted *pro hac vice*. To do so, the attorney must submit an application, Certificate of Good Standing, and $50 filing fee.

Address
Clerk, U.S. District Court, District of Arizona
401 W. Washington St., Room 130
Phoenix, AZ 85003

Telephone
602-322-7200
District Court Website
www.azd.uscourts.gov

Bankruptcy Court Admission

Regular: Any attorney admitted to the U.S. District Court of Arizona, may practice before this Court.

If an attorney is a member of the bar of this court but does not currently reside in Arizona, the court may require the association of resident local counsel.

Pro Hac Vice: An attorney who is not a member of the bar of the U.S. Dist. Court, Dist. of Arizona, but who is a member of the bar of another U.S. Dist. Court may upon application be permitted to appear and participate in a particular case. Unless authorized by the Constitution of the United States or an Act of Congress, an attorney is not eligible for limited admission pursuant to this rule if (i) the attorney resides in Arizona, (ii) the attorney is regularly employed in Arizona or (iii) the attorney is regularly engaged in the practice of law in Arizona. Unless otherwise ordered, the applicant shall designate in the application local counsel currently residing in Arizona. The application shall state whether the applicant has filed with this court any other applications for limited admission or *pro hac vice* applications within 1 year preceding the application. No fee.

Bankruptcy Court Website
www.azb.uscourts.gov

Telephone
602-682-4000

U.S. District Court – California Central District

Authorized Active Judges	Circuit
28	9

U.S. Courthouse. Photo: U.S. GSA by Carol M. Highsmith, Inc.

Admission

State Bar Membership Required	California
Automatic Admission with State Bar Membership	No
Additional Test Required	No
Certificate of Good Standing Required	No, unless for *pro hac vice*
Sponsor Required	No
Oath Required	Yes
Fee	$200 if admitted to CA bar less than 3 years; $250 if admitted 3+ years.

Pro Hac Vice Admission

Any person who is not otherwise eligible for admission to practice before this Court, but who is a member of any U.S. Court, the District of Columbia Court of Appeals, or the court of any State, Territory or Insular Possession of the United States, may, upon application and in the discretion of the Court, be permitted to participate *pro hac vice* in a particular case.

The person seeking to appear *pro hac vice* is required to designate an attorney who is a member of the Bar of this Court and who maintains an office within this District as local counsel with whom the Court and opposing counsel may readily communicate regarding the conduct of the case unless otherwise ordered by the Court.

$275 fee for each case.

Address
United States District Court
Central District of California
312 North Spring Street, Room 529
Los Angeles, CA 90012

Telephone
213-894-2085

District Court Website
www.cacd.uscourts.gov

Bankruptcy Court Admission

Regular: An attorney admitted to the district court may practice before the bankruptcy court.

Pro Hac Vice: See district court *pro hac vice* admission rules above. No fee.

Bankruptcy Court Website
www.cacb.uscourts.gov

Telephone
213-894-3118

91

U.S. District Court – California Eastern District

Authorized Active Judges	Circuit
6	9

Robert T. Matsui U.S. Courthouse. Photo: U.S. Dist. Ct. Eastern California

Admission

State Bar Membership Required	California
Automatic Admission with State Bar Membership	No
Additional Test Required	No
Certificate of Good Standing Required	Yes, from State Bar of California
Sponsor Required	No
Oath Required	Yes
Fee	$180

Pro Hac Vice Admission

An attorney who is a member of any U.S. Court or bar of any State, or of any Territory or Possession of the U.S., and who has been retained to appear in this Court may, upon application and in the discretion of the Court, be permitted to participate in a particular case. Unless authorized by the Constitution of the United States or an Act of Congress, an attorney is not eligible to practice if any one or more of the following apply: (i) the attorney resides in California, (ii) the attorney is regularly employed in California, or (iii) the attorney is regularly engaged in professional activities in California.
The attorney shall also designate a member of the Bar of this Court with whom the Court and opposing counsel may readily communicate.
Submit Certificate of Good Standing from Court in the state of primary residence. $180 fee.

Address
Office of the Clerk
U.S. District Court
501 I Street, Room 4-200
Sacramento, CA 95814-7300

Telephone
916-930-4000

District Court Website
www.caed.uscourts.gov

Bankruptcy Court Admission

Regular: Members of the District Court are members of the Bankruptcy Court.
Pro Hac Vice: See District Court Rules. Submit motion on Bankruptcy Court's form along with Cert. of Good Standing from the Court in the attorney's state of primary residence and $180 fee.

Bankruptcy Court Website
www.caeb.uscourts.gov

Telephone
916-930-4400

U.S. District Court – California Northern District

Authorized Active Judges	Circuit
14	9

Philip Burton Federal Building. Photo: U.S. DOJ

Admission

State Bar Membership Required	California
Automatic Admission with State Bar Membership	No
Additional Test Required	No
Certificate of Good Standing Required	Yes (cert. of active membership in CA Bar)
Sponsor Required	No
Oath Required	Yes
Fee	$210

Pro Hac Vice Admission

An attorney who is not a member of the Bar of the Northern District of California, but who is an active member in good standing of the bar of another United States court or of the highest court of another state or the District of Columbia, may appear in an action in this district after he or she has been admitted to practice *pro hac vice*. $210 fee per case.

Address
U.S. District Court
Clerk's Office, Attn: Attorney Admissions
450 Golden Gate Avenue
San Francisco, CA 94102

Telephone
415-522-2060

District Court Website
www.cand.uscourts.gov

U.S. District Court Northern District of California Historical Society
See link on Dist. Court's homepage. 415-522-4620 or HistoricalSociety@cand.uscourts.gov

Bankruptcy Court Admission

Regular: Members of the U.S. District Court for the Northern District of California may practice before this Court.

Pro Hac Vice: See District Court *pro hac vice* admission rules above. $210 fee.

Bankruptcy Court Website
www.canb.uscourts.gov

Telephone
415-268-2300

U.S. District Court – California Southern District

Authorized Active Judges	Circuit
13	9

Admission

State Bar Membership Required	California
Automatic Admission with State Bar Membership	No
Additional Test Required	No
Certificate of Good Standing Required	No
Sponsor Required	No
Oath Required	Yes
Fee	$180

Pro Hac Vice Admission

An attorney not eligible for admission, but who is a member of the bar of any U.S. court or any state or of any territory or insular possession of the United States, and who has been retained to appear in this court, may, upon written application and in the discretion of the court, be permitted to participate in a particular case. Unless authorized by the Constitution of the United States or acts of Congress, an attorney is not eligible to practice pursuant if any one or more of the following apply to the attorney: (1) resides in California, (2) is regularly employed in California, or (3) is regularly engaged in business, professional, or other activities in California. $180 fee per case.

A judge to whom a case is assigned may in that case, in the judge's discretion, require an attorney appearing in this court pursuant to the provisions of this rule and who maintains an office outside of this district to designate a member of the bar of this court who does maintain an office within this district as co-counsel with the authority to act as attorney of record for all purposes.

Address
Clerk's Office, U.S. District Court
880 Front Street, Suite 4290
San Diego, CA 92101-8000

Telephone
619-557-5600
District Court Website
www.casd.uscourts.gov

Jacob Weinberger U.S. Courthouse. Photos: U.S. GSA; by Donna Kempner

Bankruptcy Court Admission

Regular: Members of the U.S. District Court for the Southern District of California.
Pro Hac Vice: See District Court *pro hac vice* admission rules above. $180 fee.

Bankruptcy Court Website
www.casb.uscourts.gov

Telephone
619-557-5620

U.S. District Court – Guam

Circuit
9

U.S. Courthouse. Photo: Anonymous on Wikipedia

Admission

Territory Bar Membership Required	Guam
Automatic Admission with Territory Bar	No
Additional Test Required	No
Certificate of Good Standing Required	Yes, from Supreme Court of Guam
Sponsor Required	Yes
Oath Required	Yes
Fee	$250

Pro Hac Vice Admission

An attorney who is not eligible for admission, but who is a member in good standing of, and eligible to practice before, the bar of any United States Court or of the highest court of any State or of any Territory or Insular Possession of the United States, who is of good moral character, and who has been retained to appear in this Court, may, upon written application and in the discretion of the Court, be permitted to appear and participate in a particular case.
Unless authorized by the Constitution of the United States or Acts of Congress, an attorney is not eligible to practice if any one or more of the following apply: 1) he/she resides in Guam, 2) he/she is regularly employed in Guam, or 3) he/she is regularly engaged in business, professional or other activities in Guam.
An attorney applying to practice before this Court shall designate an attorney who is an active member in good standing of the Bar of this Court, who resides in and has an office in this District, as co-counsel. $250 fee.

Address
Clerk, District Court of Guam
520 West Soledad Avenue, 4th Floor
Hagatna, GU 96910-4950

Telephone
671-473-9100
District Court Website
www.gud.uscourts.gov

Bankruptcy Court Admission

See District Court rules above for admission requirements.

Bankruptcy Court Website
www.gud.uscourts.gov (District Court site)

Telephone
671-493-9100 (District Court)

U.S. District Court – Hawaii

Authorized Active Judges	Circuit
4	9

Prince Jonah Kuhio Federal Building. Photo: U.S. FBI

Admission

State Bar Membership Required	Hawaii (for attorneys admitted after October 1, 1997)
Automatic Admission with State Bar Membership	No
Additional Test Required	No
Certificate of Good Standing Required	Yes, proof of membership in the Hawaii state bar
Sponsor Required	No
Oath Required	Yes
Fee	$225

Pro Hac Vice Admission

An attorney who is an active member in a bar of the highest court of any State or Territory of the United States or the District of Columbia, who has been retained to appear in this court, may, upon written application and in the discretion of this court, be permitted to appear and participate in a particular case pursuant to the rules.

An attorney who has been the subject of a criminal investigation known to the attorney or a criminal prosecution or conviction in any court in the past 10 years may, in this court's sole discretion, be eligible to practice provided the attorney satisfactorily explains the circumstances surrounding the criminal investigation, prosecution, or conviction.

Unless authorized by the Constitution of the United States or Acts of Congress, an attorney is not eligible to practice pursuant to this section if any one or more of the following apply: the attorney resides in Hawaii; the attorney is regularly employed in Hawaii; or the attorney is regularly engaged in business, professional, or law-related activities in Hawaii.

The attorney shall also designate in the application a member in good standing of the bar of this court who maintains an office within the district to serve as associate counsel. $225 fee.

Address
Clerk, U.S. District Court
300 Ala Moana Blvd.
Honolulu, HA 96850

Telephone
808-541-1300
District Court Website
www.hid.uscourts.gov

Bankruptcy Court Admission

Regular: The local rules of practice of the District Court regarding attorney admission and practice generally apply in all bankruptcy cases and proceedings.

Pro Hac Vice: Attorneys may request permission to appear *pro hac vice* in a bankruptcy proceeding by filing an application substantially conforming to the local form. $225 fee.

Bankruptcy Court Website
www.hib.uscourts.gov

Telephone
808-522-8100

U.S. District Court – Idaho

Authorized Active Judges	Circuit
2	9

James A. McClure Federal Building & U.S. Courthouse. Photo: U.S. DOJ

Admission

State Bar Membership Required	Idaho
Automatic Admission with State Bar Membership	No
Additional Test Required	No
Certificate of Good Standing Required	No
Sponsor Required	No
Oath Required	Yes
Fee	$170

Pro Hac Vice Admission

An attorney not eligible for admission, but who is a member of and eligible to practice before the bar of any United States Court or of the highest court of any state or of any territory or insular possession of the United States, who is of good moral character, and who has been retained to appear in this Court, may, upon written application and in the discretion of the Court, be permitted to appear and participate in a particular case.

The attorney filing *pro hac vice* must designate a member of the bar of this Court who maintains an office within this Court as co-counsel with the authority to act as attorney of record for all purposes. $200 fee.

Address
U.S. District Court
550 W Fort Street, Suite 400
Boise, ID 83724
Attn: Attorney Admissions

Telephone
208-334-9009

District Court Website
www.id.uscourts.gov

Bankruptcy Court Admission

Regular: Any attorney who has been admitted to practice in the Supreme Court of the State of Idaho (including one admitted by reciprocity) is eligible for admission to the bar of this court. Any attorney admitted to practice before the District Court for the District of Idaho is admitted to the bar of the bankruptcy court without further process.

Each applicant for admission shall present to the clerk a written application stating the applicant's residence and office address and by what courts the applicant has been admitted to practice and the respective dates of admission to those courts.

Pro Hac Vice: See District Court *pro hac vice* rules. $200 fee.

Bankruptcy Court Website
www.id.uscourts.gov (on Dist. Ct. site)

Telephone
208-334-1361

U.S. District Court – Montana

Authorized Active Judges	Circuit
3	9

Russell E. Smith Federal Building. Photo: National Archives, RG 121-BS, Box 55, Folder S, Print 3

Admission

State Bar Membership Required	Montana
Automatic Admission with State Bar Membership	No
Additional Test Required	No
Certificate of Good Standing Required	Yes, from State Bar of Montana
Sponsor Required	Yes
Oath Required	Yes
Fee	$250

Pro Hac Vice Admission

An attorney not eligible for admission under the rules, but who is a member of and eligible to practice before the Bar of any United States Court or of the highest court of any state or of any territory or insular possession of the United States, who is of good moral character, and who has been retained to appear in this Court, may, upon motion to and in the discretion of the presiding judge, be permitted to appear and participate in a particular case.

An applicant attorney must obtain the name, address, telephone number, and written consent of local counsel who is a member of the Bar of this Court and with whom the Court and opposing counsel may readily communicate regarding the conduct of the case. $250 fee.

Address
Clerk of Court, Attn: Attorney Admissions
P.O. Box 8537
Missoula, MT 59807

Telephone
406-542-7260
District Court Website
www.mtd.uscourts.gov

Bankruptcy Court Admission

Regular: Admission to the Bar of this Court is limited to attorneys who are members of the State Bar of Montana. The Local Rules of Procedure of the U.S. District Court for the District of Montana generally govern the admission of attorneys to practice before the U. S. Bankruptcy Court for the District of Montana.

Pro Hac Vice: An attorney not eligible for admission under the rules, but who is a member of and eligible to practice before the Bar of any United States Court or of the highest court of any state or of any territory or insular possession of the United States, who is of good moral character, and who has been retained to appear in this Court, may, upon motion to and in the discretion of the presiding judge, be permitted to appear and participate in a particular case.

Local counsel is required, unless waived by the Court. $250 fee.

Bankruptcy Court Website
www.mtb.uscourts.gov

Telephone
406-782-3354

U.S. District Court – Nevada

Authorized Active Judges	Circuit
7	9

Lloyd D. George U.S. Courthouse. Photo: U.S. DOJ

Admission

State Bar Membership Required	Nevada
Automatic Admission with State Bar Membership	No
Additional Test Required	No
Certificate of Good Standing Required	No
Sponsor Required	Yes
Oath Required	Yes
Fee	$175

Pro Hac Vice Admission

An attorney who is not a member of the bar of this court, who has been retained or appointed to appear in a particular case, may do so only with permission of the court. The attorney may submit the verified petition if the following conditions are met:
(1) The attorney is not a member of the State Bar of Nevada;   (2) The attorney is not a resident of the State of Nevada;   (3) The attorney is not regularly employed in the State of Nevada;   (4) The attorney is not engaged in substantial business, professional, or other activities in the State of Nevada;   (5) The attorney is a member in good standing and eligible to practice before the bar of any jurisdiction of the United States; and   (6) The attorney associates an active member in good standing of the State Bar of Nevada as counsel of record in the action or proceeding.
$175 fee.

Address
Clerk, U.S. District Court
District of Nevada, Room 1334
333 Las Vegas Blvd. So.
Las Vegas, NV 89101

Telephone
702-464-5400

District Court Website
www.nvd.uscourts.gov

Bankruptcy Court Admission

See District Court rules for admission. $175 fee.

Bankruptcy Court Website
www.nvb.uscourts.gov

Telephone
702-527-7000

U.S. District Court – Northern Mariana Islands

Admission

Commonwealth Bar Membership Required	Northern Mariana Islands
Automatic Admission w/ Commonwealth Bar Membership	No
Residency Requirement	Any attorney admitted to practice before this court, but who does not reside in and have a full-time, staffed office in the Northern Mariana Islands, may practice only by associating local counsel. Temporary membership available for government attorneys.
Additional Test Required	No
Certificate of Good Standing Required	Permanent: Proof of membership in Commonwealth Bar. Temporary: Any state, territory or District of Columbia
Sponsor Required	No
Oath Required	Yes, in person
Fee	$250

Pro Hac Vice Admission

Upon written application approved in the judge's discretion, an attorney who is a member in good standing of the bar of any United States court or of the highest court of any State, Territory, or Commonwealth of the United States, who is of good moral character, and who has been retained to appear in this court, may appear and participate in a particular case subject to the rules. Unless otherwise authorized by the United States Constitution or Acts of Congress, an attorney is ineligible to practice if: (i) the attorney resides in the Northern Mariana Islands; or (ii) the attorney is regularly employed in the Northern Mariana Islands, except by the CNMI government; or (iii) the attorney regularly engages in business, professional, or other activities in the Northern Mariana Islands.
The attorney shall also designate in the application a member of this court's bar with whom the court and opposing counsel may readily communicate regarding the conduct of the case.
$250 fee.

Address
Northern Mariana Islands District Court
PO Box 500687
Saipan MP 96950-0687

Telephone
670-236-2902
District Court Website
www.nmid.uscourts.gov

Bankruptcy Court Admission

See District Court rules above for admission requirements.

Bankruptcy Court Website
See District Court site

Telephone
Call District Court

U.S. District Court – Oregon

Authorized Active Judges	Circuit
6	9

Mark O. Hatfield U.S. Courthouse. Photo: U.S. DOJ

Admission

State Bar Membership Required	Oregon
Automatic Admission with State Bar Membership	No
Additional Test Required	No
Certificate of Good Standing Required	No
Sponsor Required	Yes (2)
Oath Required	Yes, in person
Fee	$200

Pro Hac Vice Admission

Any attorney who is an active member in good standing of the bar of any United States court, or the highest court of any state, territory, or insular possession of the United States, may apply to be specially admitted *pro hac vice* in a particular case, provided he or she:

(1) Associates with an attorney admitted to general practice before the bar of this Court, who will meaningfully participate in the preparation and trial of the case.

(2) Pays the $100 admissions fee and files a *pro hac vice* admission application in every case in which the attorney seeks to be specially admitted.

(3) Certifies professional liability insurance, or an equivalent financial responsibility, will apply and remain in force for the duration of the case, including any appeal proceedings.

Address
U.S. District Court of Oregon
1000 S.W. Third Ave., Suite 740
Portland, OR 97204

Telephone
503-326-8021
District Court Website
www.ord.uscourts.gov
USDC of OR Historical Society
www.usdchs.org

Bankruptcy Court Admission

Regular: To appear before the court, an attorney must be admitted to practice before the district court.

Pro Hac Vice: The district court rules for *pro hac vice* apply to the Bankruptcy Court, however, no fee shall apply.

Bankruptcy Court Website
www.orb.uscourts.gov

Telephone
503-326-1500

U.S. District Court – Washington Eastern District

Authorized Active Judges	Circuit
4	9

Thomas F. Foley U.S. Courthouse. Photo: U.S. Dist. Ct. Washington Eastern Dist.

Admission

State Bar Membership Required	Washington
Automatic Admission with State Bar Membership	No
Additional Test Required	No
Certificate of Good Standing Required	No
Sponsor Required	Yes (2). If not acquainted with 2 members of this Bar, may have sponsors from Washington State Bar or another state bar.
Oath Required	Yes
Fee	$175

Pro Hac Vice Admission

Any member of the bar of any court of the United States, or of the highest court of any state, or of any organized territory of the United States, and who neither resides nor maintains an office for the practice of law in the State of Washington, may be permitted upon a showing of particular need to appear and participate in a particular case.
Any non-admitted attorney applying to participate in a particular case shall pay the $150 application fee prescribed by the judges of this court. For good cause shown, the rule may be waived by the Court in a criminal case.
There shall be joined of record in such appearance an associate attorney having an office in this state and admitted to practice in this court who shall sign all pleadings, motions, and other papers prior to filing and shall meaningfully participate in the case.

Address
Office of the Clerk, U.S. District Court
P.O. Box 1493
Spokane, WA 99210

Telephone
509-458-3400
District Court Website
www.waed.uscourts.gov

Bankruptcy Court Admission

Regular & *Pro Hac Vice*: Any attorney who is admitted to practice to the bar of the U.S. District Court for the Eastern District of Washington is eligible to practice before this court. Matters concerning eligibility, procedure for admission, permission to practice in a particular case *pro hac vice* shall be controlled by the rules of the District Court $150 *pro hac vice* admission fee.

Bankruptcy Court Website
www.waeb.uscourts.gov

Telephone
509-458-5300

U.S. District Court – Washington Western District

Authorized Active Judges	Circuit
8	9

United States Courthouse. Photo: U.S. DOJ

Admission

State Bar Membership Required	Washington
Automatic Admission with State Bar Membership	No
Additional Test Required	No
Certificate of Good Standing Required	No
Sponsor Required	Yes (2)
Oath Required	Yes
Fee	$200

Pro Hac Vice Admission

Any member in good standing of the bar of any court of the United States, or of the highest court of any other state, or of any organized territory of the United States, and who neither resides nor maintains an office for the practice of law in the Western District of Washington normally will be permitted upon application and upon a showing of particular need to appear and participate in a particular case if there shall be joined of record in such appearance an associate attorney having an office in this district and admitted to practice in this court. Attorneys who are admitted to the bar of this court but reside outside the district need not associate with local counsel.

Address
U.S. District Court, Western District of Washington
Office of the Clerk
700 Stewart Street, Suite 2310
Seattle, WA 98101

Telephone
206-370-8862

District Court Website
www.wawd.uscourts.gov

Bankruptcy Court Admission

Regular: Attorneys who are admitted to the bar of the U.S. District Court for the Western District of Washington may practice before the bankruptcy court.

Pro Hac Vice: An attorney who neither resides nor maintains an office in the Western District of Washington normally will be permitted to participate in a case upon submitting an Application for Leave to Appear *Pro Hac Vice*. $150 fee.

Bankruptcy Court Website
www.wawb.uscourts.gov

Telephone
206-370-5200

Bankruptcy Appellate Panel for the Ninth Circuit

Richard H. Chambers Court of Appeals Building. Photo: U.S. GSA

Admission

Any attorney admitted to practice before a District Court of the Ninth Circuit or the Court of Appeals for the Ninth Circuit and who is in good standing before such court shall be deemed admitted to practice before the Bankruptcy Appellate Panel.

Pro Hac Vice Admission

An attorney not admitted as described above may apply to the Bankruptcy Appellate Panel for permission to appear in a particular appeal.

Address
U.S. Bankruptcy Appellate Panel for the Ninth Circuit
Richard H. Chambers Court of Appeals Building
125 South Grand Avenue
Pasadena, CA 91105

Telephone
626-229-7220

BAP Website
www.bap9.uscourts.gov

U.S. Court of Appeals for the Tenth Circuit

Authorized Active Judges	Circuit
12	10

Byron White U.S. Courthouse. Photos: U.S. GSA

Admission

Bar/Court Membership Required	Any state, another U.S. Court of Appeals, Supreme Court of the United States, or a U.S. District Court
Additional Test Required	No
Certificate of Good Standing Required	No, unless no Sponsor is moving application
Sponsor Required	Yes, unless providing a Certificate of Good Standing from state bar
Oath Required	Yes
Fee	$200.

Address
Office of the Clerk
U.S. Court of Appeals for the Tenth Circuit
1823 Stout Street
Denver, CO 80257

Telephone
303-844-3157

Appeals Court Website
www.ca10.uscourts.gov

U.S. District Court – Colorado

Authorized Active Judges	Circuit
7	10

Alfred A. Arraj U.S. Courthouse. Photos: U.S. GSA

Admission

State Bar Membership Required	Any state, federal territory or District of Columbia
Automatic Admission with State Bar Membership	No
Additional Test Required	No
Certificate of Good Standing Required	No
Sponsor Required	No
Oath Required	Yes
Fee	$160

Pro Hac Vice Admission

The Court **no longer offers *pro hac vice* admissions**.

Address
Clerk, United States District Court
Alfred A. Arraj U.S. Courthouse, Room A-105
901 19th Street
Denver, CO 80294-3589

Telephone
303-844-3433

District Court Website
www.cod.uscourts.gov

Bankruptcy Court Admission

Regular: An attorney admitted to practice in the U. S. District Court of Colorado is qualified to practice in this bankruptcy court, provided, regardless of whether an attorney is admitted to practice in Colorado or in the U.S. District Court for the District of Colorado, when an attorney is located outside of Colorado and does not have an office in Colorado, the court, in its sole discretion, may impose additional requirements for practice before the bankruptcy court, including that such out-of-state counsel retain qualified local counsel.

Pro Hac Vice: An attorney who is a member of the bar in any other state or any other U.S. Court, but not authorized to appear in this court, may, upon motion for admission to practice *pro hac vice*, participate in the conduct of a particular case. Such motions may be made in open court if filed within 3 court days of the hearing. Call Court Clerk for motion and local counsel requirements.

Bankruptcy Court Website
www.cob.uscourts.gov

Telephone
720-904-7300

U.S. District Court – Kansas

Authorized Active Judges	Circuit
6	10

Robert J. Dole U.S. Courthouse. Photo: U.S. DOE

Admission

State Bar Membership Required	Kansas or U.S. District Court for Western District of Missouri
Automatic Admission with State Bar Membership	No
Additional Test Required	No
Certificate of Good Standing Required	No
Sponsor Required	Yes
Oath Required	Yes
Fee	$150

Pro Hac Vice Admission

Persons not admitted to practice in this court who are members in good standing of the bar of another state, upon motion made by a member of the bar of this court in good standing, may be admitted for the purpose of a particular case only. The motion must be in writing and must include an affidavit.
A $50 *pro hac vice* registration fee is required for each case.
Local counsel is responsible for signing and filing all documents in the case.

Address
Clerk, U.S. District Court
259 U.S. Courthouse
500 State Avenue
Kansas City, KS 66101

Telephone
913-735-2229

District Court Website
www.ksd.uscourts.gov

Bankruptcy Court Admission

Regular: The bar of this court consists of those attorneys admitted to practice and in good standing now and in the future as members of the bar of the U.S. District Court for the District of Kansas
Pro Hac Vice: See District Court Rules. $50 fee.

Bankruptcy Court Website
www.ksb.uscourts.gov

Telephone
316-315-4110

U.S. District Court – New Mexico

Authorized Active Judges	Circuit
7	10

Pete V. Domenici U.S. Courthouse. Photo: U.S. Dist. Ct. New Mexico

Admission

State Bar Membership Required	New Mexico
Automatic Admission with State Bar Membership	No
Additional Test Required	No
Certificate of Good Standing Required	No
Sponsor Required	No
Oath Required	Yes
Fee	$150. Annual dues of $25.

Pro Hac Vice Admission

An attorney who is not a member of the Court may appear in an action and file and serve documents electronically under the rules. Must associate with local counsel.

Address
U.S. District Court, Clerk's Office
333 Loma Boulevard NW, Suite 270
Albuquerque, NM 87102

Telephone
505-348-2000

District Court Website
www.nmcourt.fed.us

Bar Association of the U.S. District Court for the District of New Mexico
www.nmcourt.fed.us/web/DCDOCS/Forms/USDCBarAssocApp.pdf

Bankruptcy Court Admission

Regular: An attorney admitted to practice before the U.S. District Court for the District of New Mexico is a member of the bar of this court. An attorney who is eligible for membership in the bar of the U.S. District Court for the District of New Mexico and who has applied but who has not yet been admitted, may, with leave of court, appear and plead in specific cases.

Pro Hac Vice: All attorneys residing outside the District who are members of the bar of any state may participate in a particular case or proceeding before this court without the association of a resident member of the bar of this court, provided, however, that in any case or proceeding in which the court deems it necessary for the purpose of appearance, or ready availability, or otherwise in the interest of expediting disposition of the case or proceeding, the court may require non-resident counsel to associate a resident member of the bar of this court. A non-resident attorney shall file a motion to be admitted *pro hac vice*, which shall contain the statement that the attorney is familiar with the local rules. No fee.

Bankruptcy Court Website
www.nmcourt.fed.us/usbc/

Telephone
505-348-2500

U.S. District Court – Oklahoma Eastern District

Authorized Active Judges	Circuit
2	10

Ed Edmondson U.S. Courthouse. Photo: National Archives, RG 121-BS, Box 72, Folder JJ, Print 1

Admission

State Bar Membership Required	Any state or federal
Automatic Admission with State Bar Membership	No
Additional Test Required	No
Certificate of Good Standing Required	No, unless admitted to another Oklahoma U.S. District Court
Sponsor Required	No
Oath Required	Yes
Fee	$175

Pro Hac Vice Admission

Any attorney who is eligible for admission to the board of this Court may in the discretion of a judge of this Court be granted temporary admission to practice in a pending case.
Attach to motion a Request for Admission *Pro Hac Vice* form along with $50 fee.

Address
Clerk of Court
U.S. District Court, Eastern District of Oklahoma
P.O. Box 607
Muskogee, OK 74401

Telephone
918-684-7920

District Court Website
www.oked.uscourts.gov

Bankruptcy Court Admission

Regular: All Oklahoma attorneys filing in the U.S. Bankruptcy Court for the Eastern District of Oklahoma are required to be admitted to the Eastern District.
Pro Hac Vice: For non-resident attorneys only, file a motion for admission *pro hac vice*, complete an application, submit $50 filing fee. Present a proposed order to the Bankruptcy Court Judge.

Bankruptcy Court Website
www.okeb.uscourts.gov

Telephone
918-549-7200

U.S. District Court – Oklahoma Northern District

Authorized Active Judges	Circuit
4	10

Admission

State Bar Membership Required	Any state or federal
Automatic Admission with State Bar Membership	No
Additional Test Required	No
Certificate of Good Standing Required	No, unless admitted to another Oklahoma U.S. District Court
Sponsor Required	Yes (2), unless admitted to another Oklahoma U.S. District Court
Oath Required	Yes
Fee	$200

Pro Hac Vice Admission

Any attorney who is eligible for admission to the bar of this Court may in the discretion of a judge of this Court be granted temporary admission to practice. Attorneys requesting such admission are required to attach to their motion the completed request form along with the required $75 fee.

However, the *pro hac vice* fee will be waived as a matter of course if the attorney has been approved for admission as a member in this district and awaits the next admission ceremony. If the attorney fails to appear at the next available admission ceremony, and subsequently applies for a waiver of the *pro hac vice* fee, a waiver will not be granted as a matter of course, but upon discretion of the Court.

Address
United States District Court Clerk
Northern District of Oklahoma
333 W 4th Street, Room 411
Tulsa, OK 74103

Telephone
918-699-4700

District Court Website
www.oknd.uscourts.gov

Bankruptcy Court Admission

Regular: An attorney who has been admitted to practice and remains in good standing before the **U.S. District Court for the Northern, Western, or Eastern District of Oklahoma, or before the Supreme Court of the State of Oklahoma**, may practice before this Court without special permission.

Pro Hac Vice: An attorney who has been admitted to practice before any other court of the United States, or any other State, and who is familiar with these Local Rules may practice before this Court by permission. Permission to practice before the Court may be requested by filing a motion in the main bankruptcy case (or by making an oral request during any proceeding before the Court, followed by a written motion) and paying the $75 fee to the Clerk of the U.S. District Court for the Northern District of Oklahoma.

Bankruptcy Court Website
www.oknb.uscourts.gov

Telephone
918-699-4000

U.S. District Court – Oklahoma Western District

Authorized Active Judges	Circuit
7	10

Federal Building and U.S. Courthouse. Photos: U.S. GSA by Carol M. Highsmith, Inc.

Admission

State Bar Membership Required	Any state or federal. Any attorney admitted to practice in any other U.S. District Court of Oklahoma may be admitted in this district upon the motion of a member of the Bar, in open court, without the filing of a formal motion.
Automatic Admission with State Bar Membership	No
Additional Test Required	No
Certificate of Good Standing Required	Yes, if applying based on membership in another bar/court
Sponsor Required	No
Oath Required	Yes
Fee	$175

Pro Hac Vice Admission

Any attorney who is eligible for admission to the bar of this Court may, in the discretion of a judge of this Court, be granted temporary admission to practice in a pending case. Attorneys requesting such admission are required to attach to their motion a completed Request for Admission *Pro Hac Vice* form along with the required $50 fee.

Address
U.S. District Court
Room 1210, U.S. Courthouse
200 N.W. 4th Street
Oklahoma City, OK 73102

Telephone
405-609-5000

District Court Website
www.okwd.uscourts.gov

Bankruptcy Court Admission

Regular: Members of **both** the U.S. District Court for the Western District of Oklahoma **and of the Supreme Court of the State of Oklahoma** may practice before this Court.

Pro Hac Vice: An attorney admitted before any other court of the U.S. may appear in a pending case with permission of the court subject to any conditions imposed. $50 fee.

Bankruptcy Court Website
www.okwb.uscourts.gov

Telephone
405-609-5700

U.S. District Court – Utah

Authorized Active Judges	Circuit
5	10

Frank E. Moss U.S. Courthouse. Photos: U.S. GSA by Carol M. Highsmith, Inc.

Admission

State Bar Membership Required	Utah
Automatic Admission with State Bar	No
Additional Test Required	No
Certificate of Good Standing Required	No
Sponsor Required	Yes, in person (if cannot attend, then written motion)
Oath Required	Yes
Fee	$150

Pro Hac Vice Admission

Attorneys who are not active members of the Utah State Bar but who are members in good standing of the bar of the highest court of another state or the District of Columbia may be admitted *pro hac vice* upon filing the application, paying the $15 fee, having a motion made by a member of the Court, and association with local counsel for non-residents.

Applicants who are new residents, unless otherwise ordered by the court, must state either (i) that they have taken the Utah State Bar examination and are awaiting the results, or
(ii) that they are scheduled to take the next Utah State Bar examination.

Address
U.S. District Court, Attn: Attorney Admissions
U.S. Courthouse, 350 S. Main St., Room 150
Salt Lake City, UT 84101-2180

Telephone
801-524-6100
District Court Website
www.utd.uscourts.gov

Bankruptcy Court Admission

Regular: The bar of this court consists of attorneys admitted to the District Court.

Pro Hac Vice: Attorneys who are not active members of the Utah State Bar but who are members of another state or of any federal court may appear for the purpose of participating in a meeting of creditors without leave of the court. In all other matters, such attorneys may be admitted in a case by order of the court. Applicants must file a motion for admission made by a member of the bar of this court. For nonresident applicants, unless otherwise ordered by the court, the applicant must associate with local counsel. No fee.

Bankruptcy Court Website
www.utb.uscourts.gov

Telephone
801-524-6687

U.S. District Court – Wyoming

Authorized Active Judges	Circuit
3	10

Joseph C. O'Mahoney Federal Center. Photo: U.S. Dist. Ct. Wyoming

Admission

State Bar Membership Required	Wyoming
Automatic Admission with State Bar Membership	No
Additional Test Required	No
Certificate of Good Standing Required	No
Sponsor Required	Yes
Oath Required	Yes
Fee	$200

Pro Hac Vice Admission

All attorneys who have not been admitted to practice in the courts of the State of Wyoming must seek admission *pro hac vice* based upon a motion made by a member of the Bars of the State of Wyoming and of this Court and an affidavit of the attorney seeking *pro hac vice* admission. Unless otherwise ordered, a motion to appear *pro hac vice* shall be granted only if the applicant associates with a currently licensed member of the Bars of the State of Wyoming and of this Court who shall participate in the preparation and trial of the case to the extent required by the Court. The applicant must also be a member in of the bar of another state and the bar of another federal court in order to be eligible for *pro hac vice* admission in any matter before this Court. The Wyoming member of the Bar shall move the applicant's admission at the commencement of the first hearing to be held before the Court. $100 fee.

Address
Clerk, U.S. District Court
Joseph C. O'Mahoney Federal Building
2120 Capitol Avenue, Room 2141
Cheyenne, WY 82001

Telephone
307-433-2120

District Court Website
www.wyd.uscourts.gov

Bankruptcy Court Admission

Regular: The bar of this Court consists of attorneys admitted to practice as members of the bar of the U.S. District Court for the District of Wyoming.

Pro Hac Vice: The District Court rules apply to all attorneys who appear in adversary proceedings or contested matters before this Court, unless otherwise excused from compliance. Counsel not admitted to practice before this Court may file motions without admission *pro hac vice* in an uncontested matter.

Bankruptcy Court Website
www.wyb.uscourts.gov

Telephone
307-433-2200

Bankruptcy Appellate Panel for the Tenth Circuit

Admission

An attorney is admitted to practice before this court if the attorney is:
1. Admitted to practice by and a member in good standing of the United States Court of Appeals for the Tenth Circuit; or
2. Admitted to practice by and a member in good standing of a United States District Court within the Tenth Circuit; or
3. Admitted to practice by a United States Bankruptcy Court in the case or proceeding on appeal.

Address
U.S. Bankruptcy Appellate Panel for the Tenth Circuit
Byron White U.S. Courthouse
1823 Stout Street
Denver, CO 80257

Telephone
303-335-2900

BAP Website
www.bap10.uscourts.gov

U.S. Court of Appeals for the Eleventh Circuit

Authorized Active Judges	Circuit
12	11

Elbert P. Tuttle U.S. Court of Appeals Building. Photo: LC-DIG-pplot-13737-01511

Admission

Bar/Court Membership Required	Any state, another U.S. Court of Appeals, Supreme Court of the United States, or a U.S. District Court
Additional Test Required	No
Certificate of Good Standing Required	Yes
Sponsor Required	Optional
Oath Required	Yes
Fee	$170. $10 renewal every 5 years.

Address
Attorney Admissions Clerk
U.S. Court of Appeals, Eleventh Circuit
56 Forsyth Street, N.W.
Atlanta, GA 30303

Telephone
404-335-6100

Appeals Court Website
www.ca11.uscourts.gov

Eleventh Circuit Historical Society
http://sites.google.com/site/circuit11history/home

U.S. District Court – Alabama Middle District

Authorized Active Judges	Circuit
3	11

Frank M. Johnson Jr. Federal Building & U.S. Courthouse. Photo: LC-DIG-pplot-13735-01544

Admission

State Bar Membership Required	Alabama
Automatic Admission with State Bar Membership	No
Additional Test Required	No
Certificate of Good Standing Required	Required if a member is not sponsoring the motion for admission
Sponsor Required	Required only if not submitting a Certificate of Good Standing
Oath Required	Yes
Fee	$200. Renewal fee $50 every 5 years.

Pro Hac Vice Admission

Any attorney who is not a member of this Court but who is admitted to the U.S. District Court in which such person resides or regularly practices law, may be admitted *pro hac vice* by an order of any district judge, magistrate judge, or bankruptcy judge of this Court. A certificate of good standing from the district in which the attorney is admitted must be attached to the request. Any such attorney who appears as counsel by filing any pleading or paper in any case pending in this Court shall, contemporaneously with the filing of such papers, apply for admission *pro hac vice*. $50 fee.

Address
Clerk, U.S. District Court
One Church Street, Suite B-110
Montgomery, AL 36104

Telephone
334-954-3600
District Court Website
www.almd.uscourts.gov

Bankruptcy Court Admission

Regular: The bar of this Court shall consist of all members of the bar of the U.S. District Court for the Middle District of Alabama.
Pro Hac Vice: See District Court rules. $50 fee.

Bankruptcy Court Website
www.almb.uscourts.gov

Telephone
334-954-3800

116

U.S. District Court – Alabama Northern District

Authorized Active Judges	Circuit
8	11

Hugo L. Black U.S. Courthouse. Photo: U.S. Dist. Ct. Alabama Northern Dist.

Admission

State Bar Membership Required	Alabama, and (1) who reside in Alabama or regularly engage in the practice of law in Alabama, or (2) who files a Certificate of Good Standing from another Alabama U.S. District Court
Automatic Admission with State Bar	No
Additional Test Required	No
Certificate of Good Standing Required	Only if from another U.S. Dist. Court in Alabama
Sponsor Required	Yes, unless submitting a Certificate of Good Standing from another U.S. District Court in Alabama
Oath Required	Yes
Fee	$200. $50 readmission fee every 5 years.

Pro Hac Vice Admission

Any attorney who is not a member of the bar of this court but who is admitted to practice before the U.S. District Court for the district in which (or the state in which) such person resides or regularly practices law, may, upon request and payment of the $50 fee, be allowed to appear in a case *pro hac vice* by an order of any district judge or bankruptcy judge of this court. Any such attorney who appears as counsel by filing any pleading or paper in any case in this court shall within 10 days thereafter apply to appear *pro hac vice*.

Address
Clerk, U.S. District Court
1729 5th Avenue North, Room 140
Birmingham, AL 35203

Telephone
205-278-1701
District Court Website
www.alnd.uscourts.gov

Bankruptcy Court Admission

Regular: Admission to the U.S. District Court for the Northern District of Alabama.
Pro Hac Vice: See District Court rules. $50 fee.

Bankruptcy Court Website
www.alnb.uscourts.gov

Telephone
205-714-4000

U.S. District Court – Alabama Southern District

Authorized Active Judges	Circuit
3	11

John A. Campbell U.S. Courthouse. Photo: U.S. Dist. Ct. Alabama Southern Dist.

Admission

State Bar Membership Required	Alabama
Automatic Admission with State Bar Membership	No
Additional Test Required	No
Certificate of Good Standing Required	No, unless from another U.S. Dist. Ct. in Alabama where applicant resides or regularly practices
Sponsor Required	Yes
Oath Required	Yes, in person unless submitting a Cert. of Good Standing from another U.S. Dist. Court in Alabama
Fee	$200

Pro Hac Vice Admission

Attorneys residing outside the State of Alabama may be generally admitted to practice before the U.S. District Court for the Southern District of Alabama only if they are members in good standing of the Alabama Bar, otherwise they may only be admitted *pro hac vice*.
Submit motion and Certificate of Good Standing from the federal court where applicant resides and regularly practices. If not admitted to that federal court, then from the state court where applicant resides and regularly practices. $50 fee.

Address
Clerk, U.S. District Court
Southern District of Alabama
113 St. Joseph St., Room 123
Mobile, AL 36602

Telephone
251-690-2371

District Court Website
www.als.uscourts.gov

Bankruptcy Court Admission

Regular: Admission to practice before the Bar of the U.S. District Court of the Southern District of Alabama shall constitute admission to practice before this court.
Pro Hac Vice: See District Court rules. No fee.

Bankruptcy Court Website
www.alsb.uscourts.gov

Telephone
251-441-5391

U.S. District Court – Florida Middle District

Authorized Active Judges	Circuit
15	11

Admission

State Bar Membership Required	Florida
Automatic Admission with State Bar Membership	No
Additional Test Required	No
Certificate of Good Standing Required	Only if a member of another U.S. District Court in Florida
Sponsor Required	Yes (2), unless submitting a Certificate of Good Standing from another U.S. District Court in Florida
Oath Required	Yes, in person
Fee	$165. Renewal fee of $20 every 2 years.

Pro Hac Vice Admission

Any attorney who is not a resident of Florida but who is a member of the bar of any U.S. District Court outside Florida may appear specially as counsel of record; without formal admission, provided however, such privilege is not abused by appearances in separate cases to such a degree as to constitute the maintenance of a regular practice of law in Florida; and provided further that whenever appearing as counsel by filing any pleading or paper in any case pending in this Court, a non-resident attorney shall file within 14 days a written consent-to-act on the part of some member of the bar of this Court, resident in Florida, upon whom all notices and papers may be served and who will be responsible for the progress of the case, including the trial in default of the non-resident attorney. The non-resident attorney shall comply with both the $10 fee and e-mail registration requirements, and the written designation shall certify the non-resident attorney's compliance.

In an extraordinary circumstance a lawyer who is not a member of the Middle District bar may move *instanter* for temporary admission provided the lawyer appears eligible for membership in the Middle District bar and simultaneously initiates proceedings for general or special admission to the Middle District bar. Temporary admission expires in 30 days or upon determination of the application for general or special admission, whichever is earlier.

Address
U.S. Courthouse and Federal Building Annex
United States District Court
401 W Central Blvd., Suite 1200
Orlando, FL 32801-0120

Telephone
407-835-4227

District Court Website
www.flmd.uscourts.gov

Bankruptcy Court Admission

Regular: Members of the Court are those admitted to practice in the U.S. District Court for the Middle District of Florida.

Pro Hac Vice: Any attorney residing outside the State of Florida, who is a member of the bar of any U.S. District Court other than the Middle District of Florida, may appear specially in any case without formal admission; provided, however, such privilege is not abused by frequent appearances in separate cases to such a degree as to constitute the maintenance of a regular practice of law in the Middle District of Florida. See additional local rules.

Bankruptcy Court Website
www.flmb.uscourts.gov

Telephone
813-301-5046

U.S. District Court – Florida Northern District

Authorized Active Judges	Circuit
4	11

Admission

State Bar Membership Required	Any state
Automatic Admission with State Bar Membership	No
Additional Test Required	Yes. Must take an online exam to test knowledge of Local Rules of the Northern District of Florida and the Federal Rules of Civil Procedure.
Certificate of Good Standing Required	Yes
Sponsor Required	No
Oath Required	Yes
Fee	$170

Pro Hac Vice Admission

Prior to any appearance, any attorney who is not a member of the bar of this district must request permission in writing to appear, certifying that he or she has successfully completed the computer-based tutorial on local rules of the Northern District of Florida and the computer-based tutorial on this court's CM/ECF System, available on the District's webpage. In addition, a copy of a certificate of good standing date dated within the last six months from the Florida Bar, from the bar of any state, or from the U.S. District Court to which said attorney has been admitted, together with an admission fee in the amount set by the court by administrative order, shall accompany said request. Upon completion of these requirements the attorney will be admitted to the bar of this district. With the advent of electronic case filing, **this court no longer draws any substantive distinction between membership in the bar of this district and *pro hac vice* admission**. An attorney admitted *pro hac vice* will be treated as a member of the bar of this district and will remain a member, even after termination of the case, until such time as the attorney affirmatively withdraws from the bar of this district or no longer meets the admission qualifications.

Address
Attorney Admissions Clerk
U.S. District Court
111 N. Adams St., Suite 322
Tallahassee, FL 32301-7717

Telephone
850-521-3531

District Court Website
www.flnd.uscourts.gov

Bankruptcy Court Admission

The U.S. District Court for the Northern District of Florida governs the admission and appearance of attorneys before the Bankruptcy Court. All attorneys admitted to practice or approved to appear *pro hac vice* in the United States District Court for the Northern District of Florida are by virtue thereof admitted to practice in the Bankruptcy Court.

Bankruptcy Court Website
www.flnb.uscourts.gov

Telephone
850-521-5001

U.S. District Court – Florida Southern District

Authorized Active Judges	Circuit
18	11

David W. Dyer Federal Building & U.S. Courthouse. Photo: National Archives, RG 121-BS, Box 15, Folder R, Print 1

Admission

State Bar Membership Required	Florida
Automatic Admission with State Bar Membership	No
Additional Test Required	Yes. Applicants must pass a Core Exam with a score of at least 80%. At least 40 questions are derived from the Federal Rules of Civil and Criminal Procedures, Evidence and Jurisdiction/Venue and 10 questions from the Southern District of Florida Local Rules.
Cert of Good Standing Required	Yes, from Florida Bar.
Sponsor Required	No
Oath Required	Yes
Fee	$175

Pro Hac Vice Admission

Local counsel must file papers, enter appearance for parties, sign stipulations or sign and receive payments on judgments, decrees or orders. Must designate local counsel.
No more than 3 appearances in a 365-day period. $75 fee.

Address
U.S. District Court
400 North Miami Avenue, Room 8N09
Miami, FL 33128-7716

Telephone
305-523-5100
District Court Website
www.flsd.uscourts.gov

Bankruptcy Court Requirements

Be a member of the Bar of the U.S. District Court for the Southern District of Florida.
Read and remain familiar with the rules, administrative orders, the Federal Rules of Bankruptcy Procedure, the Federal Rules of Civil Procedure, the Federal Rules of Evidence, the Florida Bar's Rule of Professional Conduct, and the Bankruptcy Code.
Earn at least 12 credit hours from the Florida Bar for attending or participating in CLE courses related to the subject area of "Bankruptcy Law" during each attorney's Florida Bar three-year CLE reporting requirement. No fee for *pro hac vice* admission.

Bankruptcy Court
www.flsb.uscourts.gov

Telephone
305-714-1800

Bankruptcy Bar Assn S. Dist FL
www.bbasdfl.org

U.S. District Court – Georgia Middle District

Authorized Active Judges	Circuit
4	11

William Augustus Bootle Federal Building & Courthouse. Photo: U.S. Dist. Ct. Georgia Middle Dist.

Admission

State Bar Membership Required	Georgia
Automatic Admission with State Bar Membership	No
Additional Test Required	No
Certificate of Good Standing Required	No, except for *pro hac vice* admission
Sponsor Required	No
Oath Required	Yes
Fee	$175

Pro Hac Vice Admission

If applicant is not a member of the State Bar of Georgia and do not maintain an office in Georgia, he/she must obtain a Certificate of Good Standing from the US District Court where he/she is admitted to practice. $100 fee per case.

Address
U.S. District Court, Middle District of Florida
Attn: Attorney Admissions Clerk
P.O. Box 128
Macon, GA 31202

Telephone
478-752-3497

District Court Website
www.gamd.uscourts.gov

Bankruptcy Court Admission

See District Court rules for regular and *pro hac vice* admission requirements.

Bankruptcy Court Website
www.gamb.uscourts.gov

Telephone
478-752-3506

U.S. District Court – Georgia Northern District

Authorized Active Judges	Circuit
11	11

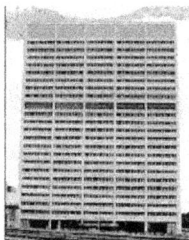

Richard B. Russell Federal Building & U.S. Courthouse. Photo: U.S. DOJ

Admission

State Bar Membership Required	Georgia
Automatic Admission with State Bar Membership	No
Additional Test Required	No
Certificate of Good Standing Required	No
Sponsor Required	Yes (2), one in person
Oath Required	Yes, in person
Fee	$150

Pro Hac Vice Admission

Non-resident attorney who is not an active member of the State Bar of Georgia, but who is a member in good standing of the bar of any United States court or of the highest court of any State may apply in writing for permission to appear *pro hac vice*. $150 fee.
An attorney applying to appear *pro hac vice* must designate a local member of the bar of this court with whom the opposing counsel and the court may communicate regarding the conduct of the case and upon whom papers shall be served. Attorneys sponsoring applicant have a duty to verify their bar admission of record status.

Address
U.S. District Court, Northern District of Florida
2211 U.S. Courthouse
75 Spring Street, S.W.
Atlanta, GA 30303-3361

Telephone
404-215-1600

District Court Website
www.gand.uscourts.gov

Bankruptcy Court Admission

Regular: Any attorney who is admitted to the bar of the U.S. District Court for the Northern District of Georgia is admitted to the bar of the Bankruptcy Court.
Pro Hac Vice: A non-resident attorney who is not an active member in good standing of the State Bar of Georgia, but who is a member in good standing of the bar of any United States Court or of the highest court of any State may apply in writing for permission to appear *pro hac vice*. An attorney applying to appear *pro hac vice* must also designate a local member of the bar of the Bankruptcy Court with whom the opposing counsel and the Bankruptcy Court may readily communicate regarding the conduct of the case and upon whom papers shall be served. $150 fee.

Bankruptcy Court Website
www.ganb.uscourts.gov

Telephone
404-215-1000

123

U.S. District Court – Georgia Southern District

Authorized Active Judges	Circuit
3	11

Tomochichi Federal Building & U.S. Courthouse. Photo U.S. GSA by Walter Smalling

Admission

State Bar Membership Required	Georgia
Automatic Admission with State Bar Membership	No
Additional Test Required	No
Certificate of Good Standing Required	No
Sponsor Required	Yes (2)
Oath Required	Yes, in person
Fee	$200

Pro Hac Vice Admission

Georgia bar members who reside in this district or maintain their principal place of business in this district shall not appear before this Court via *pro hac vice* admission, but instead must join this Court's bar, even to represent someone in one (or an occasional) case. Any attorney not subject to the preceding sentence but who is a member of another federal district court, may be permitted to appear and participate in a particular case before this Court, whether civil or criminal, with the prior approval of this Court, subject to designating local counsel and filing a Certificate of Good Standing from another federal court. $200 fee.

Address
Clerk, U.S. District Court
125 Bull Street, 3rd Floor
Savannah, GA 31402

Telephone
912-650-4020
District Court Website
www.gasd.uscourts.gov

Bankruptcy Court Admission

Regular: Any attorney who is admitted to the bar of the U.S. District Court for the Southern District of Georgia is admitted to the bar of the Bankruptcy Court.

Pro Hac Vice: Any attorney who is not admitted shall be permitted to appear and participate in a bankruptcy case or proceeding only upon compliance the District Local Rules for Attorneys, and payment of the prescribed $200 fee for admission *pro hac vice*.

Bankruptcy Court Website
www.gasb.uscourts.gov

Telephone
912-650-4100

U.S. Court of Appeals for the District of Columbia Circuit

Authorized Active Judges	Circuit
11	DC

E. Barrett Prettyman U.S. Courthouse. Photo: U.S: PO

Admission

Bar/Court Membership Required	Any state, another U.S. Court of Appeals, Supreme Court of United States, or a U.S. District Court
Additional Test Required	No
Certificate of Good Standing Required	Yes
Sponsor Required	Yes (2)
Oath Required	Yes
Fee	$200

Address
Office of the Clerk
U.S. Court of Appeals, District of Columbia Circuit
333 Constitution Avenue, NW
Washington, DC 20001-2866

Telephone
202-216-7300

Appeals Court Website
www.cadc.uscourts.gov

U.S. District Court – District of Columbia

Authorized Active Judges	Circuit
15	DC

Admission

District Bar/Court Membership Required	District of Columbia or the state in which applicant maintains principal law office and is a member of a U.S. District Court that provides for reciprocal admission to this Court.
Automatic Admission with District Membership	No
Additional Test Required	No
Certificate of Good Standing Required	No
Sponsor Required	Yes
Oath Required	Yes
Fee	$175. Renew membership every 3 years for $25.

Pro Hac Vice Admission

An attorney who is not a member of the Bar of this Court may be heard in open court only by permission of the judge to whom the case is assigned. Any attorney seeking to appear *pro hac vice* must file a motion signed by a sponsoring member of the Bar of this Court.

Address
Attorney Admissions
U.S. District and Bankruptcy Courts
333 Constitution Avenue, N.W., Room 1225
Washington, D.C. 20001

Telephone
202-354-3000

District Court Website
www.dcd.uscourts.gov

Bankruptcy Court Admission

Regular: To practice in the Bankruptcy Court, an attorney must be admitted to the District Court Bar, and that is the bar of this Court.

Pro Hac Vice: An attorney who is a member in good standing of the bar of any U.S. Court or of the highest Court of any State, but who is not a member of the bar of this Court, may file papers in this Court only if such attorney joins of record a member in good standing of the bar of this Court. All papers submitted by non-members of the bar of this Court must be signed by such counsel and by a member of the bar of this Court joined in compliance with this Rule. An attorney who is not a member of the bar of this Court may be heard in open court only by permission of the judge to whom the case is assigned. No fee.

Bankruptcy Court Website
www.dcb.uscourts.gov

Telephone
202-354-3000

Alien Terrorist Removal Court

Must be duly empowered by the Attorney General to practice before this court and represent the government, or be appointed as a special attorney by the judge. Appeals are heard by the U.S. Court of Appeals for the District of Columbia. Counsel that represented the alien in the Alien Terrorist Removal Court must continue to represent the alien in an appeal without additional appointment.

Address
E. Barrett Prettyman U.S. Courthouse
333 Constitution Avenue, N.W., Room 3219
Washington, DC 20001

Telephone
202-354-3050

U.S. Court of Appeals for the Federal Circuit

Authorized Active Judges	Circuit
12	Federal

Admission

Bar/Court Membership Required	Any state, another U.S. Court of Appeals, Supreme Court of United States, U.S. Court of International Trade, U.S. Court of Federal Claims, U.S. Court of Appeals for Veterans Claims, or a U.S. District Court
Additional Test Required	No
Certificate of Good Standing Required	No, unless there is no Sponsor moving application
Sponsor Required	Yes, unless providing a Certificate of Good Standing
Oath Required	Yes
Fee	$200

Address
Clerk of Court
U.S. Court of Appeals for the Federal Circuit
717 Madison Place, NW, Room 401
Washington, DC 20439

Telephone
202-275-8000

Appeals Court Website
www.cafc.uscourts.gov

Federal Circuit Bar Association
www.fedcirbar.org

Federal Circuit Historical Society
www.federalcircuithistoricalsociety.org

U.S. Court of Federal Claims

Admission

Bar/Court Membership Required	Any U.S. state, territory, possession or District of Columbia
Additional Test Required	No
Certificate of Good Standing Required	Yes
Sponsor Required	Yes, 2 members of the bar of this Court or the United States Supreme Court
Oath Required	Yes, in person
Fee	$250

Pro Hac Vice Admission

An attorney may participate *pro hac vice* in any proceeding before this court if: (A) the attorney is admitted to practice before the highest court of any U.S. state, territory, or possession or the District of Columbia; and (B) the attorney of record for any party has requested and is present for such participation and has received the court's approval.
Foreign Attorneys. (A) *In General.* Any person qualified to practice in the highest court of any foreign state may be specially admitted to practice before this court but only for purposes limited to a particular case; such person may not serve as the attorney of record. (B) *Procedures.* A member of the bar of this court must file with the clerk a written motion to admit the applicant at least 7 days prior to the court's consideration of the motion. In the case of such an admission, an oath and fee are not required.

Address
Clerk of Court
U.S. Court of Federal Claims
717 Madison Place, NW, Room 103
Washington, DC 20005

Telephone
202-357-6400

Court Website
www.uscfc.uscourts.gov

Court of Federal Claims Bar Association
www.cfcbar.org

U.S. Court of International Trade

James L. Watson Court of International Trade. Photo: LC-DIG-pplot-13816-01589

Admission

Bar/Court Membership Required	Any state, territory or District of Columbia, United States Supreme Court, any U.S. Court of Appeals or any U.S. District Court
Additional Test Required	No
Certificate of Good Standing Required	No, unless submitting without a Sponsor that has known applicant for more than one year
Sponsor Required	Yes, unless submitting Certificate of Good Standing
Oath Required	Yes
Fee	$50. $50 renewal every 5 years.

Address
United States Court of International Trade
Admissions Office – Room 299
One Federal Plaza
New York, NY 10278-0001

Telephone
212-264-2812
Court Website
www.cit.uscourts.gov

Customs and International Trade Bar Association
http://citba.org

U.S. Court of Appeals for Veterans Claims

Admission

Bar/Court Membership Required	Attorneys: Any state, District of Columbia, territory, U.S. Supreme Court Non-Attorneys: Under direct supervision of attorney or employed by eligible Veterans organization
Additional Test Required	No
Certificate of Good Standing Required	Attorneys: Yes
Sponsor Required	Attorneys: No Non-Attorneys: Yes, CEO of eligible employer
Oath Required	Yes
Fee	$100

Address
Admissions Clerk
U.S. Court of Appeals for Veterans Claims
625 Indiana Avenue, NW, Suite 900
Washington, DC 20004

Telephone
202-501-5970

Court Website
www.uscourts.cavc.gov

Court of Appeals for Veterans Claims Bar Association
www.cavcbar.net

U.S. Tax Court

U.S. Tax Court Building. Photo: U.S. GSA by Carol M. Highsmith, Inc.

Admission

Bar/Court Membership Required	Attorneys: Any U.S. state, territory, commonwealth or District of Columbia Non-attorneys: None
Additional Test Required	Attorneys: No Non-attorneys: Yes, to test applicant's knowledge of (1) the Tax Court Rules of Practice and Procedure, (2) Federal taxation, (3) the Federal Rules of Evidence, and (4) legal ethics, including ABA Model Rules of Professional Conduct
Certificate of Good Standing Required	Attorneys: Yes Non-attorneys: No
Sponsor Required	Attorneys: No Non-attorneys: Yes (2)
Oath Required	Yes
Fee	$35 Non-attorneys also pay $75 exam fee

Address
Admissions Office
U.S. Tax Court
400 Second Street, N.W., Room 111
Washington, DC 20217

Telephone
202-521-4629

Court Website
www.ustaxcourt.gov

Foreign Intelligence Surveillance Court of Review

U.S. District Court or Court of Appeals judges are appointed by the Chief Justice of the Supreme Court of the United States to this Court. If the Court upholds a denial of the government's application, the government may file a petition for certiorari with the Supreme Court of the United States.

Foreign Intelligence Surveillance Court

U.S. District Court judges are appointed by the Chief Justice of the Supreme Court of the United States to this Court. Appeals are heard by the Foreign Intelligence Court of Review.

Admission

Bar/Court Membership Required	Any United States Court
Additional Requirement	Must be duly empowered by the Attorney General to practice before this court and represent the government (Department of Justice)

Address
E. Barrett Prettyman U.S. Courthouse
333 Constitution Avenue, N.W., Room 3219
Washington, DC 20001

Telephone
202-357-6200

U.S. Judicial Panel on Multidistrict Litigation

Admission

Bar/Court Membership Required	Any U.S. District Court
Automatic Admission with Bar Membership	Every member in good standing of the Bar of any district court of the United States **is entitled without condition** to practice before the Judicial Panel on Multidistrict Litigation. Any attorney of record in any action transferred under 28 U.S.C. § 1407 may continue to represent his or her client in any district court of the United States to which such action is transferred. Parties to any action transferred under § 1407 are not required to obtain local counsel in the district to which such action is transferred.
Additional Test Required	No
Certificate of Good Standing Required	No
Sponsor Required	No
Oath Required	No
Fee	None

Address
U.S. Judicial Panel on Multidistrict Litigation
Thurgood Marshall Federal Judiciary Building
One Columbus Circle, NE
Room G-255, North Lobby
Washington, DC 20002

Telephone
202-502-2800

Panel Website
www.jpml.uscourts.gov

U.S. Court of Appeals for the Armed Forces

Admission

Bar/Court Membership Required	Any state or federal
Additional Test Required	No
Certificate of Good Standing Required	Yes
Sponsor Required	No
Oath Required	Yes
Fee	$35

Address
Clerk of the Court
United States Court of Appeals for the Armed Services
450 E Street, NW
Washington, DC 20442-0001

Telephone
202-761-7364

Court Website
www.armfor.uscourts.gov

Judge Advocates Association
www.jaa.org

Air Force Court of Criminal Appeals

Admission

Bar/Court Membership Required	Any state or federal
Additional Test Required	No
Certificate of Good Standing Required	Yes
Sponsor Required	No
Oath Required	Yes
Fee	None

Address
United States Air Force Court of Criminal Appeals
112 Luke Avenue, Suite 343
Bolling Air Force Base
Washington, DC 20032

Telephone
202-767-1550

Court Website
http://afcca.law.af.mil

Army Court of Criminal Appeals

Admission

Bar/Court Membership Required	Any state or federal
Additional Test Required	Yes
Certificate of Good Standing Required	Yes, unless certified by a Judge Advocate General pursuant to Article 26(b) or 27(b)(1) of the Uniform Code of Military Justice.
Sponsor Required	Yes, in person
Oath Required	Yes, in person. Must sign the Roll Book.
Fee	None

Address
Clerk of Court
U.S. Army Judiciary (JALS-CC)
901 North Stuart Street, Suite 1200
Arlington, VA 22203-1837

Telephone
703-588-7908

Navy-Marine Corps Court of Criminal Appeals

Admission

Bar/Court Membership Required	Any state or federal
Additional Test Required	No
Certificate of Good Standing Required	Yes, for civilian attorneys
Sponsor Required	No
Oath Required	Yes
Fee	None

Address
Clerk of Court
Navy-Marine Corps Court of Criminal Appeals
1254 Charles Morris St., SE
Suite 320
Washington Navy Yard, DC 20374-5124

Telephone
202-685-7700

Court Website
www.jag.navy.mil/nmcca.htm

Coast Guard Court of Criminal Appeals

Admission

Bar/Court Membership Required	Any state or federal. See *Pro Hac Vice* rules below.
Additional Test Required	No
Certificate of Good Standing Required	Yes
Sponsor Required	No
Oath Required	Yes
Fee	None

Pro Hac Vice Admission

The court assigns military counsel. If it can be shown the defendant sought to add the civilian attorney to his/her legal defense team and the civilian attorney is a member in good standing of another bar, he/she may be admitted *pro hac vice* for that case.

Address
4200 Wilson Blvd.
Suite 790, STOP 7160
Arlington, VA 20598-7160

Telephone
202-493-1147

Court Website
www.uscg.mil/legal/cca/Court_of_Criminal_Appeals.asp

Other Territorial & Freely Associated State Courts

District of Columbia Court of Appeals

District Bar/Court Membership Required	Any state or territory (1) for 5 years immediately preceding the application, or (2) having passed a written bar exam and received 133+ on Multistate Bar Examination and 75+ on Multistate Professional Responsibility Exam
Test Required	Yes, if not already qualified under category above. Essay, MBE and MPRE.
Certificate of Good Standing Required	Yes, if applying based on admission in another jurisdiction.
Sponsor Required	No
Oath Required	Yes
Fee	$400 based on admission in another jurisdiction. See fees if taking new examination.

Address
District of Columbia Court of Appeals
Committee on Admissions
430 E Street NW, Room 123
Washington, DC 20001

Telephone
202-879-2710

Court Website
www.dcappeals.gov

District of Columbia Bar
www.dcbar.org

* The District of Columbia Court of Appeals is equivalent to a state supreme court for the District of Columbia which is a federal district and the U.S. Capitol.

Commonwealth of Puerto Rico Supreme Court

- See also District Court for Puerto Rico under First Circuit.

Test Required	Exams given twice a year. Ongoing CLE requirement for members.
Certificate of Good Standing Required	No
Sponsor Required	No
Oath Required	Yes
Fee	$250 exam fee

Address
Executive Director
Commonwealth of Puerto Rico Supreme Court
P.O. Box 9022392
San Juan, PR 00902-2392

Telephone
787-289-0170

Court Website
www.ramajudicial.pr

Colegio de Abogados de Puerto Rico (Puerto Rico Bar Association)
www.capr.org

* This Court is equivalent to a state supreme court.

Supreme Court of the U.S. Virgin Islands

- See also District Court of the U.S. Virgin Islands under Third Circuit.

Territory Bar/Court Membership Required	Yes
Additional Test Required	Yes. See rules for transferability of MBE and MPRE. Local law essay test required.
Certificate of Good Standing Required	Yes
Sponsor Required	No
Oath Required	Yes
Fee	$350 plus other expenses.

Pro Hac Vice Admission

The attorney making the motion before the Court must be regularly admitted to practice in the Virgin Islands, an active member in good standing in the Virgin Islands Bar.
The attorney seeking *pro hac vice* admission must be currently in good standing as an active member of the bar of any state or territory of the United States or of any foreign country.
Current Certificates of Good Standing bearing the original seal of the highest court from each jurisdiction to which he or she is admitted. (Letter validating membership from a bar association in and of itself is not sufficient.)
The attorney seeking *pro hac vice* admission must have been retained or requested to represent any party in any legal matter in the Virgin Islands.
All appropriate membership dues and licensing fees must be paid by the attorney seeking *pro hac vice* admission prior to the granting of the Petition for *pro hac vice* admission.

Address
Supreme Court of the Virgin Islands
P.O. Box 590
St. Thomas, VI 00804

Telephone
340-774-2237

Court Website
www.visupremecourt.org

Virgin Islands Bar Association
www.vibar.org

* This Court is equivalent to a state supreme court.

Guam Supreme Court

- See also District Court of Guam under Ninth Circuit

Territory Bar/Court Membership Required	Yes, but may apply for temporary active membership if admitted to another state or federal bar for 5+ years.
Additional Test Required	Yes. Bar Exam or Attorney Exam
Certificate of Good Standing Required	Yes
Sponsor Required	No, except for *pro hac vice*.
Oath Required	Yes
Fee	$375 for temporary active member if admitted for 5 years in another state or federal court. Or $1,125 for attorney exam.

Pro Hac Vice Admission

An "out-of-state" lawyer is a person not admitted to practice law in Guam but who is admitted in another state, territory, or commonwealth of the United States or the District of Columbia and not disbarred or suspended from practice in any jurisdiction. [Sponsor required]
An out-of-state lawyer is "eligible" for admission *pro hac vice* if that lawyer: (A) lawfully practices solely on behalf of the lawyer's employer and its commonly owned organizational affiliates, regardless of where such lawyer may reside or work; or (B) neither resides nor is regularly employed at an office in Guam; or (C) resides in Guam but (i) lawfully practices from offices in one or more other states and (ii) practices no more than temporarily in Guam, whether pursuant to admission *pro hac vice* or in other lawful ways.
Application for permission to appear *pro hac vice* has non-refundable fee of **$1,000**.

Address
Clerk, Supreme Court of Guam
Suite 300, Guam Judicial Center
120 West O'Brien Drive
Hagåtña, Guam 96910

Telephone
671-475-3120
Court Website
www.guamsupremecourt.com
Guam Bar Association
http://guambar.org

* This Court is equivalent to a state supreme court.

Commonwealth of the Northern Mariana Islands Supreme Court

- See also United States District Court for the Northern Mariana Islands under Ninth Circuit.

Commonwealth Bar Membership Required	Yes, unless admitted in another state or territory for 5 of last 12 years.
Additional Test Required	Yes. Attorney exam: 6 essays and Multistate Performance Test. MPRE required within last 3 years.
Certificate of Good Standing Required	Yes, all jurisdictions where admitted.
Fee	Attorney applicant $450

Address
Bar Admissions Administrator
Commonwealth Supreme Court
P.O. Box 502165
Saipan, MP 96950

Telephone
670-236-9800
Court Website
www.justice.gov.mp
CNMI Bar Association
www.cnmibar.net

* This Court is equivalent to a state supreme court.

High Court of American Samoa

Admission

Territory Bar Membership Required	Must be admitted to any State or Territory court of the United States or of a foreign country where the English common law forms substantially the basis of that country's jurisprudence, and where English is the language of instruction and practice in the courts; provided that such prior Bar admission was premised upon proof of graduation from an accredited law school and successful completion of a bar examination or of equivalent indicia of learning and ability.
Reciprocity	The fact that an applicant has practiced for a period of 2 years or more before the highest court in a State or Territory of the United States, or of a foreign country where the English common law forms substantially the basis of that country's jurisprudence, where English is the language of instruction and practice in the courts of that jurisdiction, and which State, Territory, or country extends reciprocity to American Samoa is prima facie evidence of the applicant's fitness to practice law in American Samoa and to be admitted to the Bar on reciprocity, reserving to the Standing Committee the power to review such circumstances as necessary.
Additional Test Required	No
Residency	The Court has concluded the Rules "do not specifically set forth any length of time for resident prior to seeking admission to practice, it is clear that one must, of course, be a resident in order to apply for admission" to the Bar. Any person admitted to the Bar who is not a judge and who does not practice law in American Samoa may be an inactive member. Applications for admission to active membership made by non-resident attorneys from other states have been denied.
Oath Required	Yes
Fee	$100 application fee. Up to $125 investigation fee. Active members: $75 annual bar dues. Inactive members: $35 annual bar dues.

Pro Hac Vice Admission

A person who is not a member of the American Samoa Bar but who is a member of any State or Territory court of the United States or of a foreign country where the English common law forms substantially the basis of that country's jurisprudence, where English is the language of instruction and practice in the courts of that jurisdiction and which state, Territory, or country allows members of the American Samoa Bar to appear *pro hac vice*, may at the discretion of the Chief Justice, be permitted, upon written application, to appear as counsel *pro hac vice*. However, an active member of the American Samoa Bar Association must be associated as Attorney of Record, upon whom service of process may be made and with whom the judge and opposing counsel may communicate concerning the action. $10 fee.

Address
High Court of American Samoa
Post Office Box 309
Pago Pago, American Samoa 96799

Telephone
684-633-4131
American Samoa Bar Association
www.asbar.org

Republic of the Marshall Islands Supreme Court

Republic Bar/Court Membership Required	Must be 21 years of age or older and either: (1) Be a government attorney or work for a non-profit that provides legal services to the people of the Marshall Islands who cannot afford such services. Admission under this section expires after such qualifying service ends, but then attorney can apply for admission based on this experience. (2) Apply to take the written bar examination.
Additional Test Required	Yes, unless admitted under Section 1 above. The exam is scheduled at such times and places as the Court shall designate.
Certificate of Good Standing Required	Yes, copies from **all** jurisdictions where admitted
Sponsor Required	No, but various types of references required
Oath Required	Yes
Fee	$250. $50 annual fee.

Pro Hac Vice Admission

The Supreme Court or the High Court may upon an attorney's oral or written motion and payment of a $250 non-refundable application fee grant an attorney who is licensed to practice by and is in good standing before all the courts of any other nation, or state of another nation, but who is not admitted to the practice of law in the Republic, permission to participate in the conduct of a particular case in a court of the Republic of the Marshall Islands in which such a case is pending or is to be filed. Provided, however, such motion shall be allowed only if the interests of justice will be served; and provided further, that such attorney associates with an attorney or trial assistant who ordinarily resides in the Republic and who is admitted to practice in that court, if such local counsel is available.
The local attorney or trial assistant shall at all times participate in a meaningful way in the preparation and trial of such case.

Address
Clerk of the Courts
Marshall Islands Judiciary
P.O. Box B
Majuro, MH 96960
Republic of the Marshall Islands

Telephone
692-625-2301

Court Website
http://rmicourts.org

* The Republic of the Marshall Islands is a sovereign state that entered into a Compact of Free Association with the United States.

Federated States of Micronesia Supreme Court

Territory Bar/Court Membership Required	Yes. Each applicant shall be a resident or domiciliary of the Federated States of Micronesia, or a Federated States of Micronesia citizen.
Additional Test Required	Yes. The written examination may cover any legal issue relevant to the practice of law within the Federated States of Micronesia but will concentrate upon Federated States of Micronesia constitutional law, Federated States of Micronesia statutory law, Micronesian customary law, criminal law, legal ethics, evidence, admiralty, legal research, Federated States of Micronesia procedural rules, and administrative law.
Certificate of Good Standing Required	Yes
Sponsor Required	Yes, to attest to applicant's trial experience.
Fee	$25

Pro Hac Vice Admission

The Court will consider, on a case by case basis, applications to practice in specific cases.
The Court will consider, among other things: the likelihood that granting of the motion may delay proceedings, because of communication or transportation problems; whether the movant, if not a resident of the Federated States of Micronesia, will be affiliated with local counsel knowledgeable about the litigation and capable of appearing at pre-trial and other preliminary proceedings; whether the movant, if a resident of the Federated States of Micronesia, is moving as expeditiously as possible to obtain certification as an attorney within the Federated States of Micronesia; the availability of other counsel; the complexity of the case; whether there had been prior professional association of the attorney with the client; the proof adduced of good character, competence, and admission in other jurisdictions; and any other factors indicating whether the granting of the motion would be in the interests of justice.
An attorney admitted to practice before this Court who does not reside or maintain an office within the Federated States of Micronesia in which particular litigation is pending, may be required to associate with an attorney or trial counselor admitted to practice before the Court who resides or maintains an office within the State.

Address
FSM Supreme Court – Pohnpei
P.O. Box PS-J, Palikir Station
Pohnpei FM 96941

Telephone
691-320-2357

Court Website
www.fsmlaw.org

* The Federated States of Micronesia is a sovereign state that entered into a Compact of Free Association with the United States.

Republic of Palau Supreme Court

Republic Bar/Court Membership Required	Yes
Additional Test Required	Yes. 4 part test: MBE, MPRE, MEE and Palau essay exam. May transfer MBE (scaled score of 120+), MPRE (scaled score of 75+) and state essay that was passed (to fulfill MEE requirement) from tests within the past 5 years. Must take Palauan-based Essay exam on Palau customary law, land law, the Constitution, statutes, the Compact of Free Association and case law. Score of 65+ required. Exam fee is $100. Exam offered in July.
Certificate of Good Standing Required	Yes
Sponsor Required	No
Oath Required	Yes
Fee	$200. $200 annual fee for active; $100 annual fee for inactive.

Pro Hac Vice Admission

An attorney not admitted to practice before the courts of the Republic of Palau may, on motion, be admitted for the special purpose of handling a particular case by the Justice before whom the case is pending.
Any motion made under this rule must be accompanied by a $100 special appearance fee.

Address
Clerk of Court
Palau Supreme Court
P.O. Box 248
Koror, Palau PW 96940

Telephone
680-488-2607

Bar Association Website
www.palaubar.org

* The Republic of Palau is a sovereign state that entered into a Compact of Free Association with the United States.

APPENDIX

Regional Circuit Courts of Appeal Admissions

Circuit Court of Appeals	Bar/Court Membership Required	Circuit Bar Sponsor Required	State Bar Certificate of Good Standing Required	Oath	Exam	Fee
First	Any state or federal	Yes	Yes	Yes	No	$200
Second	Any state or federal	Yes	Yes	Yes	No	$190. Renew every 5 years for $25
Third	Any state or federal	Yes	Yes	Yes	No	$190
Fourth	Any state or federal	Yes	No	Yes	No	$170
Fifth	Any state or federal	Yes	Yes	Yes	No	$200
Sixth	Any state or federal	Yes, unless prov. Cert. of Good Standing	Only required when there is no sponsor	Yes	No	$200
Seventh	Any state or federal	Yes	No	Yes	No	$165
Eighth	Any state or federal	Yes	No	Yes	No	$190
Ninth	Any state or federal	Yes, unless member of a Dist Ct in 9th Cir. and provide Cert. of Good Standing	Only required when there is no sponsor	Yes	No	$190
Tenth	Any state or federal	Yes, unless you provide a Cert. of Good Standing from any state bar	Only required when there is no sponsor	Yes	No	$200
Eleventh	Any state	Optional	Yes	Yes	No	$170. Renew every 5 years for $10
Dist. of Columbia	Any state or federal	Yes (2)	Yes	Yes	No	$200

U.S. District Court Admissions – First Circuit

District Court	Bar/Court Membership Required	District Bar Sponsor Required	Cert. of Good Standing Required	Oath	Exam	Fee	Pro Hac Vice Option
Maine	Maine	Yes	No	Yes	No	$150	Yes
Massachusetts	Massachusetts	No	Yes	Yes	No	$200	Yes
New Hampshire	New Hampshire	Typically not	No	Yes	No	$180	Yes
Puerto Rico	Any state or federal	Yes	Yes	Yes	Yes	$300	Yes
Rhode Island	Rhode Island	No	Yes	Yes	No; course	$150	Yes

U.S. District Court Admissions – Second Circuit

District Court	Bar/Court Membership Required	District Bar Sponsor Required	Cert. of Good Standing Required	Oath	Exam	Fee	Pro Hac Vice Option
Connecticut	Connecticut or any US Dist Ct	Yes (2)	Yes	Yes	No	$160	Yes
New York Eastern	New York or certain US Dist Cts	Yes	Yes, each state	Yes	No	$170	Yes
New York Northern	Any state or federal	Yes	Yes	Yes	No	$150	Yes
New York Southern	New York or certain US Dist Cts	Yes	Yes	Yes	No	$185	Yes
New York Western	New York or any state if also member of US Dist Ct in that state	Yes	Depends	Yes	No	$200	Yes
Vermont	Vermont or any US Dist Ct within the 1st or 2nd Circuit	Yes	No	Yes	No	$150	Yes

2011 Edition by John Okray   © Lawyerup Press LLC

U.S. District Court Admissions – Third Circuit

District Court	Bar/Court Membership Required	District Bar Sponsor Required	Cert. of Good Standing Required	Oath	Exam	Fee	*Pro Hac Vice* Option
Delaware	Delaware	Yes	No	Yes	No	$165	Yes
New Jersey	New Jersey	No	No	Yes	No	$200	Yes
Pennsylvania Eastern	Pennsylvania	Yes	No	Yes	No	$175	Yes
Pennsylvania Middle	Pennsylvania	Yes	No	Yes	No	$175	Yes
Pennsylvania Western	Pennsylvania, U.S. Supreme Court of any U.S. Dist Ct.	Yes	No	Yes	No	$160	Yes
Virgin Islands	Virgin Islands	Yes	No	Yes	No	None	Yes

U.S. District Court Admissions – Fourth Circuit

District Court	Bar/Court Membership Required	District Bar Sponsor Required	Cert. of Good Standing Required	Oath	Exam	Fee	*Pro Hac Vice* Option
Maryland	Any state/DC. See details.	Yes	No	Yes	No	$175	Yes
North Carolina Eastern	North Carolina	Yes, see details	No, see details	Yes	No	$180	Yes
North Carolina Middle	North Carolina	Yes, see details	No, see details	Yes	No	$150	Yes
North Carolina Western	North Carolina	Yes, see details	No, see details	Yes	No	$250	Yes
South Carolina	South Carolina	Yes (2)	No	Yes	Experience req.	$150	Yes
Virginia Eastern	Virginia, see details	Yes	Bar Card	Yes	No	$150	Yes
Virginia Western	Virginia, see details	Yes (2)	No	Yes	No	$150	Yes
West Virginia Northern	West Virginia	Yes	No	Yes	No	$150	Yes
West Virginia Southern	West Virginia	Yes	No	Yes	No	$150	Yes

2011 Edition by John Okray   © Lawyerup Press LLC

U.S. District Court Admissions – Fifth Circuit

District Court	Bar/Court Membership Required	District Bar Sponsor Required	Cert. of Good Standing Required	Oath	Exam	Fee	*Pro Hac Vice* Option
Louisiana Eastern	Louisiana	Yes (2)	No	Yes	No	$150	Yes
Louisiana Middle	Louisiana	Yes (2)	Yes	Yes	No	$180	Yes
Louisiana Western	Louisiana	Yes (2)	Yes	Yes	No	$175	Yes
Mississippi Northern	Mississippi	Yes	Yes	Yes	No	$160	Yes
Mississippi Southern	Mississippi	Yes	Yes	Yes	No	$160	Yes
Texas Eastern	Any state or federal	Yes, see details	No	Yes	No	$150	Yes
Texas Northern	Any state or DC	Yes	Yes	Yes	No	$175	Yes
Texas Southern	Any state, DC or territory	Yes (2)	Yes	Yes	No	$150	Yes
Texas Western	Any state, see details	Yes, see details	Yes	Yes	No	$170	Yes

2011 Edition by John Okray   © Lawyerup Press LLC

U.S. District Court Admissions – Sixth Circuit

District Court	Bar/Court Membership Required	District Bar Sponsor Required	Cert. of Good Standing Required	Oath	Exam	Fee	*Pro Hac Vice* Option
Kentucky Eastern	Kentucky	Yes	No	Yes	No	$180	Yes
Kentucky Western	Kentucky	Yes	No	Yes	No	$180	Yes
Michigan Eastern	Any state, DC or US Dist Ct.	No	Yes	Yes	No	$200	No, see details
Michigan Western	Any state	Yes, see details	Yes	Yes	No	$200	No, see details
Ohio Northern	Any state, DC or US Dist Ct	Yes (2)	Yes	Yes	Seminar	$190	Yes, see details
Ohio Southern	Ohio, see details	Yes (2), see details	No	Yes	Yes	$150	Yes
Tennessee Eastern	Any state or DC	Yes (2)	Yes, see details	Yes	No	$160	Yes
Tennessee Middle	Tennessee	Yes (2)	No	Yes	No	$200	Yes
Tennessee Western	Any state or DC	Yes	No	Yes	No	$150	Yes

2011 Edition by John Okray   © Lawyerup Press LLC

U.S. District Court Admissions – Seventh Circuit

District Court	Bar/Court Membership Required	District Bar Sponsor Required	Cert. of Good Standing Required	Oath	Exam	Fee	*Pro Hac Vice* Option
Illinois Central	Any state or DC	Yes, see details	No, see details	Yes	No	$185	No, see details
Illinois Northern	Any state or DC	Yes (2), see details	Yes	Yes	See details	$150+	Yes
Illinois Southern	Any state or DC	Yes	Yes	Yes	No	$200	Yes
Indiana Northern	Any state or US Supreme	Yes	Yes, each state	Yes	No	$160	Yes
Indiana Southern	Any state or US Supreme	Yes	Yes	Yes	No	$160	Yes
Wisconsin Eastern	Any state, DC or federal	No, see details	Yes	Yes	No	$185	No
Wisconsin Western	Any state, DC or federal	Yes	No	Yes	No	$150	Yes

U.S. District Court Admissions – Eighth Circuit

District Court	Bar/Court Membership Required	District Bar Sponsor Required	Cert. of Good Standing Required	Oath	Exam	Fee	*Pro Hac Vice* Option
Arkansas Eastern	Any state, see details	See details	Yes	Yes	No	$160	Yes
Arkansas Western	Any state, see details	See details	Yes	Yes	No	$160	Yes
Iowa Northern	Iowa	Yes (2)	No	Yes	No, see details	$150	Yes
Iowa Southern	Iowa	Yes (2)	No	Yes	No, see CLE.	$150	Yes
Minnesota	Minnesota	Yes	No	Yes	No	$175	Yes
Missouri Eastern	Any state or DC	Yes (2)	Yes, each state/fed	Yes	No	$200	Yes
Missouri Western	Missouri, see details	Yes (2)	No	Yes, see details	No	$157	Yes
Nebraska	Any state	No	Yes	Yes	No	$150	Yes
North Dakota	Any state or federal	No	No	Yes	No	$200	Yes
South Dakota	South Dakota	Yes	No	Yes	No	$200	Yes

2011 Edition by John Okray   © Lawyerup Press LLC

U.S. District Court Admissions – Ninth Circuit

District Court	Bar/Court Membership Required	District Bar Sponsor Required	Cert. of Good Standing Required	Oath	Exam	Fee	*Pro Hac Vice* Option
Alaska	Alaska	No	Yes	Yes	No	$250	Yes
Arizona	Arizona	Yes	No	Yes	No	$180	Yes
California Central	California	Yes	No	Yes	No	$200+	Yes
California Eastern	California	No	Yes	Yes	No	$180	Yes
California Northern	California	No	Yes	Yes	No	$210	Yes
California Southern	California	No	No	Yes	No	$180	Yes
Guam	Guam	Yes	Yes	Yes	No	$250	Yes
Hawaii	Hawaii	No	Yes	Yes	No	$225	Yes
Idaho	Idaho	No	No	Yes	No	$170	Yes
Montana	Montana	Yes	Yes	Yes	No	$250	Yes
Nevada	Nevada	Yes	No	Yes	No	$175	Yes
Northern Mariana Is.	Northern Mariana Is.	No	See details	Yes, in person	No	$250	Yes
Oregon	Oregon	Yes (2)	No	Yes	No	$200	Yes
Washington Eastern	Washington	Yes (2), see details	No	Yes	No	$175	Yes
Washington Western	Washington	Yes (2)	No	Yes	No	$200	Yes

2011 Edition by John Okray   © Lawyerup Press LLC

U.S. District Court Admissions – Tenth Circuit

District Court	Bar/Court Membership Required	District Bar Sponsor Required	Cert. of Good Standing Required	Oath	Exam	Fee	Pro Hac Vice Option
Colorado	Any state, DC or federal	No	No	Yes	No	$160	No
Kansas	Kansas, see details	Yes	No	Yes	No	$150	Yes
New Mexico	New Mexico	No	No	Yes	No	$150	Yes
Oklahoma Eastern	Any state or federal	No	No, see details	Yes	No	$175	Yes
Oklahoma Northern	Any state or federal	Yes (2), see details	No, see details	Yes	No	$200	Yes
Oklahoma Western	Any state or federal	No	Yes	Yes	No	$175	Yes
Utah	Utah	Yes	No	Yes	No	$150	Yes

U.S. District Court Admissions – Eleventh Circuit

District Court	Bar/Court Membership Required	District Bar Sponsor Required	Cert. of Good Standing Required	Oath	Exam	Fee	Pro Hac Vice Option
Alabama Middle	Alabama	No	Yes	Yes	No	$200	Yes
Alabama Northern	Alabama, see details	Yes	No, see details	Yes	No	$200	Yes
Alabama Southern	Alabama	Yes	No, see details	Yes, see details	No	$200	Yes
Florida Middle	Florida	Yes (2), see details	No, see details	Yes	No	$165	Yes
Florida Northern	Any state	No	Yes	Yes	Yes	$170	No
Florida Southern	Florida	No	Yes	Yes	Yes	$175	Yes
Georgia Middle	Georgia	No	No	Yes	No	$175	Yes
Georgia Northern	Georgia	Yes (2)	No	Yes	No	$150	Yes
Georgia Southern	Georgia	Yes (2)	No	Yes	No	$200	Yes
Wyoming	Wyoming	Yes	No	Yes	No	$200	Yes

2011 Edition by John Okray   © Lawyerup Press LLC

U.S. District Court Admissions – District of Columbia Circuit

District Court	Bar/Court Membership Required	District Bar Sponsor Required	Cert. of Good Standing Required	Oath	Exam	Fee	Pro Hac Vice Option
District of Columbia	DC or any state, see details	Yes	No	Yes	No	$175	Yes

U.S. Subject-Matter Specific Court Admissions

Court	Bar/Court Membership Required	Court Sponsor Required	Certificate of Good Standing Required	Oath	Exam	Fee
Court of Appeals for the Federal Circuit	Any state or federal	Yes, unless providing cert. of good standing.	No, unless there is no sponsor moving application	Yes	No	$200
Court of International Trade	Any state or federal	Yes, unless providing cert. of good standing.	No, unless submitting without a sponsor	Yes	No	$50
Court of Federal Claims	Any state or federal	Yes	Yes	Yes	No	$250
Tax Court	Attorneys: Any state, territory or District of Columbia.	2 required for non-attorney applicants.	Only for attorneys.	Yes	Only for non-attorneys	$35

2011 Edition by John Okray   © Lawyerup Press LLC

Military-Related Courts Admissions

Court	Bar/Court Membership Required	Court Sponsor Required	Certificate of Good Standing Required	Oath	Exam	Fee
Court of Appeals for the Armed Forces	Any state or federal	No	Yes	Yes	No	$35
Court of Appeals for Veterans Claims	Any state or federal (for attorneys). Non-attorneys may be admitted in certain instances.	Optional. For non-attorney need supervising attorney or CEO of approved Veterans Group.	Yes (for attorneys)	Yes	No	$100
Air Force Court of Criminal Appeals	Any state or federal	No	Yes	Yes	No	None
Army Court of Criminal Appeals	Any state or federal	Yes, in person	Yes	Yes	No	None
Coast Guard Court of Criminal Appeals	Any state or federal	No	Yes	Yes	No	None
Navy-Marine Corp Court of Criminal Appeals	Any state or federal	No	Yes (for non-military attorneys)	Yes	No	None

2011 Edition by John Okray   © Lawyerup Press LLC

Other Associations

The following is a list of national legal organizations that may be of interest.

Federal Bar Association
www.fedbar.org

Federal Court Clerks Association
www.fcca.ws

National Conference of Bankruptcy Clerks
www.ncbcimpact.org

Federal Judges Association
www.federaljudgesassoc.org

National Conference of Bankruptcy Judges
www.ncbj.org

Federal Magistrate Judges Association
www.fedjudge.org

American Bar Association
www.abanet.org

American Inns of Court
www.innsofcourt.org

Defense Research Institute
www.dri.org

Judge Advocates Association
www.jaa.org

United States Court Reporters Association
www.uscra.org